THE
MAYA
WORLD

THE
MAYA
WORLD

Revised Edition

Elizabeth P. Benson

THOMAS Y. CROWELL COMPANY

New York   *Established 1834*

TITLE PAGE PICTURE: Head from a sculpture relief panel at Palenque (drawing by A. P. Maudslay).

Designed by Judith Woracek Barry

Manufactured in the United States of America

Library of Congress Cataloging in Publication Data
Benson, Elizabeth P
  The Maya world.

  Bibliography: p.
  Includes index.
  1. Mayas—Antiquities.   2. Mexico—Antiquities.
3. Central America—Antiquities.   I. Title.

F1435.B47 1977   972   77–4955
ISBN 0–690–01673–5
ISBN 0–8152–0423–X   (Apollo edition)

1 2 3 4 5 6 7 8 9 10

The author is grateful to Farrar, Straus & Giroux, Inc., for permission to quote from *The Discovery and Conquest of Mexico* by Bernal Díaz del Castillo, translated by A. P. Maudslay. Copyright © 1956 by Farrar, Straus & Cudahy.

In the preparation of this book, I am indebted to the writings of many authors, especially Robert S. Chamberlain, William R. Coe, Sylvanus Morley, Tatiana Proskouriakoff, Ralph R. Roys, William T. Sanders, A. Ledyard Smith, Alfred M. Tozzer, Gordon R. Willey, and, of course, Bishop Landa. My grateful thanks go to Gordon Ekholm and Michael D. Coe, who made helpful suggestions on the manuscript; to Mrs. Margaret Sevcenko, who assisted in its preparation; to Herbert Anthony, who made the maps; and to Mrs. Katherine Edsall, Richard Amt, and Wallace Lane, who went to a great deal of trouble with the photographs. I would especially like to note my gratitude to John S. Thacher for allowing me to use the Dumbarton Oaks Pre-Columbian library and other facilities, and to express my appreciation for the inspiration and material provided by the Robert Woods Bliss Collection.

Elizabeth P. Benson

CONTENTS

A CHRONOLOGICAL CHART

Nomadic peoples	10,000 B.C.
Food-gatherers	7000 B.C.
First signs of village life	3500 B.C.

PRE-CLASSIC

Early	1500–800 B.C.
Middle	800–300 B.C.
Late	300 B.C.–A.D. 300

CLASSIC

Early	A.D. 300–600
Late	A.D. 600–900

POST-CLASSIC

	A.D. 900–1517

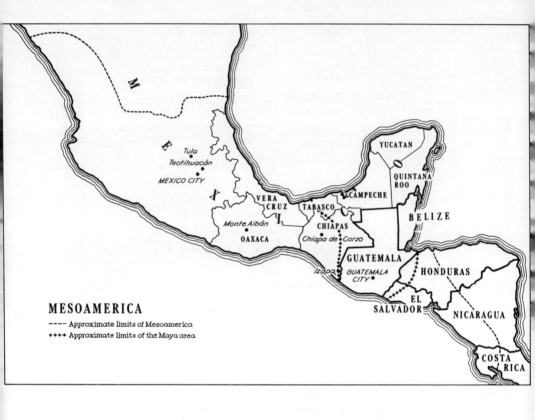

M
E
X
I
C
O

Tula
Teotihuacán
MEXICO CITY

Monte Albán
OAXACA

VERA
CRUZ

TABASCO

CHIAPAS
Chiapa de Corzo

Izapa

GUATEMALA
CITY

CAMPECHE

YUCATAN

QUINTANA
ROO

BELIZE

GUATEMALA

HONDURAS

EL
SALVADOR

NICARAGUA

COSTA
RICA

MESOAMERICA

---- Approximate limits of Mesoamerica
++++ Approximate limits of the Maya area

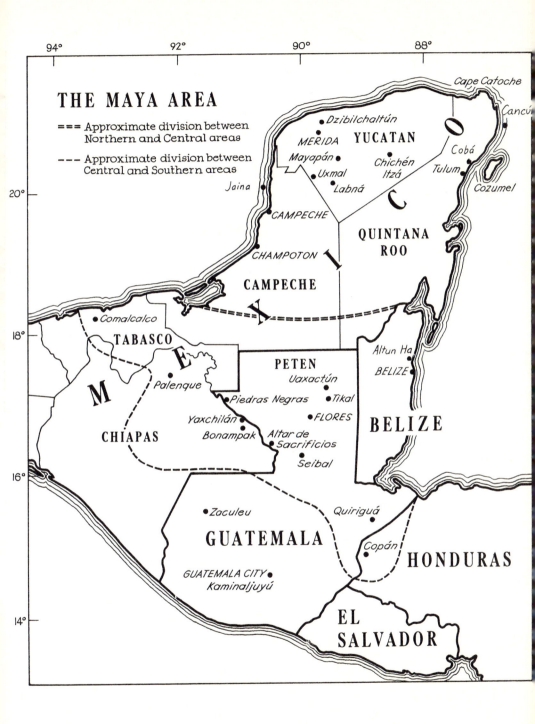

THE MAYA AREA

=== Approximate division between
Northern and Central areas

--- Approximate division between
Central and Southern areas

Cape Catoche

Cancú

Dzibilchaltún

YUCATAN

MERIDA

Mayapán

Chichén Itzá

Cobá

Uxmal

Tulum

Jaina

Labná

Cozumel

C

CAMPECHE

QUINTANA ROO

CHAMPOTON

I

CAMPECHE

X

Comalcalco

TABASCO

PETEN

Altun Ha

BELIZE

E

Palenque

Uaxactún

M

Piedras Negras

Tikal

Yaxchilán

BELIZE

CHIAPAS

Bonampak

FLORES

Altar de Sacrificios

Seibal

Zaculeu

Quiriguá

GUATEMALA

Copán

HONDURAS

GUATEMALA CITY
Kaminaljuyú

EL
SALVADOR

THE
MAYA
WORLD

I.
THE PUZZLE AND
THE PUZZLERS

Since the beginning of the sixteenth century, when the Spaniards first encountered the descendants of the ancient Maya and saw with astonishment the ruins of their great buildings, the mystery of the Maya has intrigued travelers and scholars. The civilizations of the Aztecs and the Incas, the dominant people in the New World at the time of the Spanish conquest, fascinated the more sensitive Spaniards as they have fascinated generations of later people with a romantic turn of mind. But of all the New World civilizations that existed before the arrival of the Spaniards, it is that of the Maya that appeals most to the imagination.

The Maya have existed as a people for perhaps two millennia, but their greatest period was from about A.D. 300 to 900. During this time they inhabited a large and geographically varied area that included the entire Yucatán peninsula and a periphery extending into the Mexican states of Chiapas and Tabasco on the west, the mountains of Guatemala on the south, and Honduras on the east. The heart of this area was the tropical rain forest of northern Guatemala, where the unevenly brilliant Maya civilization thrived for more than six hundred years and then, for reasons still unknown, died out.

The Maya were a paradoxical people. They cleared the jungle and built magnificent pyramided cities of stone. They produced sculpture and paintings of high esthetic quality, as well as handsomely decorated pottery and books of pounded-bark paper. They carved long hieroglyphic inscriptions on monuments in a writing so complex that it has not yet been fully deciphered. They used a mathematical notation system more sophisticated than that of their European contemporaries. They counted time past in hundreds of thousands of years, noted the movements of the planet Venus, and predicted eclipses of the sun and moon. Yet they never invented the wheel, that most basic of civilized mankind's accomplishments, and they worked with only primitive stone tools and manpower. Technologically they were a Stone Age people. This combination of intellectual and esthetic sophistication with technical primitivism is the hallmark of the Maya character.

The mysteries of the Maya civilization—the reasons for its rise, its accomplishments during its great period, the causes of its decline—still puzzle archaeologists and scholars who, especially in the last century, have used all the tools and techniques at their disposal in trying to reconstruct Maya life.

One of the best sources of information about ancient Asian, African, and European peoples has been the writings they left behind. The Maya were the only people in the Americas who had a developed form of writing, but as has already been pointed out, thus far their inscriptions cannot be entirely deciphered. Part of the problem is the limited number of texts; only three or four pre-Spanish Maya books, or codices, are known to exist. There are hundreds of stone monuments with hieroglyphic texts, but much work is still to be done before they can be completely read. Moreover, they seem to furnish only a limited kind of material.

Early Spanish arrivals in the New World wrote accounts of their adventures there, but these accounts are not only slanted from a European point of view, they were written more than six hundred years after the great period of Maya history was finished and the cities had been abandoned or taken over by other people. Some of these early accounts are the memoirs of Spanish adventurers, written in the tranquillity of old age. Sometimes information was gathered by the priests, primarily for the purpose of aiding the Church in the conversion of the newly discovered heathens. In the late sixteenth century, the King of Spain sent out a questionnaire to the Spanish land barons in the New World in which he inquired about such things as the climate, mountains and rivers, trees, plants, and animals, place names, distances between towns, the history of ancient governments, wars, and trade. The answers to these questionnaires are the *Relaciones,* which are useful early sources on the area.

The best of the early Spanish accounts of the Maya is the work of Diego de Landa, who came to Yucatán in 1549 and was later made its first bishop. Landa appears as a very contradictory character in the history of Maya studies. He wrote a long descriptive treatise on Yucatán, its people, and the way of life he found there in which he gave modern scholars their start on deciphering Maya hieroglyphs. Yet he was also responsible for an auto-da-fé in which a large number of Maya books were burned because they contained "nothing but superstition and falsehoods of the devil." Thus he destroyed what might have been valuable information on the Maya, and material that would have been helpful in the work on the Maya hieroglyphs.

A few native texts survive from the Spanish colonial period. The Spanish priests were concerned with teaching the Indians to write their own language, using Latin characters. Although it was not the purpose of the project, much native material was thus preserved. Many of these texts consist of legends or rituals that had probably come down by word of mouth. The *Popol Vuh*, a manuscript written shortly after the Conquest by a Quiché Maya Indian in highland Guatemala, gives the history and mythology of his people. The *Books of Chilam Balam*, which date from the seventeenth and eighteenth centuries, although they are surely copies of earlier manuscripts, come from Yucatán and are a mixture of history and prophecy, ritual and mythology. There are also a number of shorter manuscripts: some of them set forth ritual, some describe customs and medical lore, and there are several Maya-Spanish dictionaries. Something of the Maya can also be learned from the pre-Conquest and early colonial writings of nearby areas—for example, the great work of the Friar Sahagún on the Aztecs—for by extension these writings tell something about the Maya. But other than these small groups of texts, there are no written records that describe the Maya world at the moment of its contact with Spain, much less its great earlier period.

Europeans at the time of the Conquest tried to relate the extraordinary civilizations found in the Americas to the European world or to a world that Europeans knew about; they could not believe that these civilizations were not transplanted from somewhere else. During the centuries since the Conquest, the Indians have been variously identified as Israelites, Canaanites, Assyrians, Egyptians, Phoenicians, Carthaginians, Trojans, Greeks, Etruscans, Romans, Scythians, Tartars, Chinese Buddhists, Koreans, Hindus, African Mandingos, Madagascans, Irish, Welsh, Norse, Basques, Portuguese, French, Spaniards, Huns, or survivors of the lost continents of Atlantis or Mu.

Carved stone panel from Tikal showing Maya hieroglyphic writing and bar-and-dot numerals.

The earliest theory was that they were one of the Lost Tribes of Israel. Bishop Landa wrote that, according to some of the old people of Yucatán, their ancestors had said that the land was occupied by a race of people who came from the east by twelve paths that God had opened for them through the sea. Landa therefore concluded that these people must be Israelites. This theory had many adherents in the sixteenth and seventeenth centuries, and even today some of the best archaeological work in the area is being done with the idea of proving this. The New World Archaeological Foundation, carrying on important excavations in Mexico, is supported by the Mormon church.

That the Indians were descendants of survivors of the lost continent of Atlantis was another theory advanced in the sixteenth century. In legend, Atlantis was a great island in the Atlantic Ocean that was destroyed by volcanic eruptions, earthquakes, and tidal waves, and sank forever below the sea. Advocates of this theory believe Atlantis to be the common ancestral home of the peoples of both Egypt and the New World.

In the eighteenth and nineteenth centuries, with a revival of interest in ancient Greece and Egypt, theories were put forward connecting the American Indian with the Old World. There are books of this period that describe the Phoenician settling of America. Several books from the end of the eighteenth century maintain that Amerindians were descendants of Noah and that America was the place where the ark was built. Another favorite theory was that America had been settled by shipwrecked sailors, and still another states that it was colonized by survivors of a fleet of Alexander the Great that was wrecked in the fourth century B.C. Another supposition is that the Inca empire of South America was founded by crews from Kublai Khan's ships that had been driven across the Pacific by a great storm that wrecked the major part of the fleet the khan sent against the Japanese in the thirteenth century.

The exotic civilizations of the Americas attracted colorful characters with vivid imaginations. One of the most vociferous proponents of the Egyptian hypothesis was an imaginative man named Augustus Le-Plongeon, a doctor from the Island of Jersey whose beard and imagination were equally impressive. LePlongeon explored Yucatán, excavated there, and wrote a book called *Queen Moo and the Egyptian Sphinx* explaining how the Egyptians and the Maya came to be related.

Most of these theories, insofar as they had any factual basis, were built on comparable culture traits. For example, both Egyptians and the Maya had pyramids, hieroglyphic writing, and relief sculpture. Similar-sounding words were also used as arguments (although modern linguistic experts explain that a certain percentage of words may sound alike in a comparison of any two languages). LePlongeon, having constructed his Egyptian comparison, went on to state that one-third of Maya was pure Greek. And further, he said that there were also words in Maya that were from the Assyrian. Dr. LePlongeon believed that not only was the handwriting on the wall at Belshazzar's feast of Maya derivation, but that the last words of Jesus on the cross were Maya.

Once this game is started, it can be continued almost indefinitely. Another theory stated that Quetzalcóatl, the Mexican folk hero, was really an apostle or disciple of Christ. (Quetzalcóatl has also been identified with Atlas, Wotan, Osiris, Dionysius, Bacchus, and Poseidon.) A painting from a Mexican codex was interpreted by another theorizer as a depiction of the scene of Cain killing Abel. On the other hand, the native American population was cited in the mid-eighteenth century as a proof that not all the human race is descended from Adam and Eve. Reasoning that man could not have traversed the immense seas before the invention of the mariner's compass, proponents of this theory argued that since the Americas were clearly peopled before the time of that invention, the inhabitants of the New World are therefore not indebted to Adam and Eve.

In 1822 the first book on Maya archaeology was published in London. It was a report dating from 1787, written by a Spanish army officer who had gone into the large Maya city of Palenque, taken down all the partitions he could find, and cleared blocked doors and windows. "By dint of perseverance I effected all that was necessary to be done, so that ultimately there remained neither a window nor a doorway blocked up; a partition that was not thrown down, nor a room, corridor, court, tower, nor subterranean passage in which excavations were not effected from two to three yards in depth," he bragged. The modern archaeologist, who painstakingly sifts dirt and wants to note the position of every stone and every potsherd, is horrified by his destructiveness. The Spanish officer, incidentally, thought that the Romans—or possibly the Phoenicians or Greeks—had come to Palenque to teach the Indians to make such buildings as he found there.

When he was an undergraduate at Oxford, the Irish Lord Kingsborough saw a Mexican manuscript in the Bodleian Library that so fascinated him that he dedicated his life to collecting material about the Indians, convinced that they were one of the Lost Tribes of Israel. His nine folio volumes, published between 1831 and 1848, included one of the Maya manuscripts. Quite aside from theories, the recording of this material was an important contribution to New World studies. The ambitious project proved to be too much for Kingsborough's pocketbook, and he died in a Dublin debtor's prison.

Scouting for material in Mexico for Lord Kingsborough was a colorful Frenchman named Jean Frédéric, Count de Waldeck. Waldeck as a very young man had explored Africa; then he had studied with the foremost painters of the day in Paris just before the French Revolution. He became a soldier, and was attached as an artist to Napoleon's Egyptian campaign. After the French defeat in 1801, Waldeck explored Africa again, and later served as a naval officer in the Indian Ocean, preying on British shipping. He fought in the liberation of Chile, and ended up in Guatemala in 1821. At a time when many men would be thinking of a comfortable retirement, Waldeck began to explore Maya ruins and sketch Maya remains. He spent many of the next years in Mexico. He was a skillful artist, but sometimes his drawings had little relationship to the objects he was representing. Considered "fanciful" by his more conscientious contemporaries, he reconstructed the ruins on paper as he drew. He was killed in a street accident in Paris at the age of 109, reportedly because he had turned to look at a pretty girl.

In the nineteenth century, foreigners began to travel into the Maya area. These were intrepid travelers, for they had to combat the hazards of jungle trails, mud, disease, insects, and revolutionists in order to explore the mysterious ruins. Some of them gave excellent accounts of what they found. One was John Lloyd Stephens, an American, who, with his English artist-friend, Frederick Catherwood, visited more than forty Maya sites. Two books resulted from their travels, *Incidents of Travel in Central America, Chiapas, and Yucatan* and *Incidents of Travel in Yucatan*. These two books, published in 1841 and 1843, were best-sellers, the first one running through twelve editions in the first year. Unlike virtually all his contemporaries, Stephens did not indulge in speculation about the exotic origins of the Indians, and his descriptions are simple and clear. One envies Stephens his first view of the great Maya site of Copán, a desolate, deserted city in the solemn stillness of the jungle, where he found strange and beautiful sculptures. There were no guidebooks at that time; it was fresh ground, and Stephens knew it. He describes Catherwood standing in mud, with gloves on to protect his hands from mosquitoes, having great difficulty in depicting the designs on the Maya monuments because they were so complex and their subjects so entirely new and unintelligible. Catherwood rendered these sculptures, so differ-

A stucco relief sculpture in the Temple of the Lion at Palenque. Very little of this relief now exists.

Stone stela and altar representing a skeletal face in the Great Plaza at Copán.

ent from anything he had seen before, with such skill and openminded-ness that his drawings are still useful today. He did not see in them vestiges of other cultures; he saw them as something new.

The French Abbé Brasseur de Bourbourg, another important nineteenth-century figure, learned the Maya languages then spoken in Guatemala and was responsible for saving many early colonial manu-scripts from destruction when the Mexican monastic orders were sup-pressed. He found and preserved the manuscripts of Bishop Landa and discovered part of one of the extant pre-Conquest Maya codices. He also found, in a secondhand bookstall in Mexico, the manuscript of an impor-tant Maya-Spanish dictionary, and he published a French translation of the *Popol Vuh*. The abbé, however, in his later years, subscribed to the theory that the civilizations of Egypt and the Old World came from the New World, where they had previously been brought by colonists from the lost continent of Atlantis.

The most significant of the nineteenth-century students of the area was the Englishman, Alfred Maudslay, who spent thirteen years toward the end of the century exploring and carefully describing Maya sites, making superb photographs of the ruins, drawing accurate plans, and copying hieroglyphic inscriptions and sculpture designs. Maudslay was the first man to approach the area with a truly scientific outlook. His set of five volumes on Maya sites remains one of the finest contributions to Maya archaeology.

Maudslay worked with the expeditions that the Peabody Museum of Harvard University sent to the great Maya site of Copán in Honduras from 1891 through 1895—the same site which had so impressed Stephens and Catherwood fifty years earlier. The Peabody Museum continued to work at other sites in the Maya area, and in the next twenty years many of the Peabody explorations were carried out by an Austrian-born natu-ralized American, Teobert Maler, who had gone to Mexico with the Emperor Maximilian in 1864 as an Austrian army officer. After the execu-tion of Maximilian, Maler wandered through the forests of the Maya region with a camera, photographing ruins. For years he traveled alone through the jungles, indifferent to weather and discomfort, a capable, lonely eccentric.

Harvard has continued to work and publish its findings from the Maya area, and since the beginning of the century many other institu-tions have worked there as well. In 1915 the Carnegie Institution of Washington began work in the area, where it excavated and published its findings for many years. In subsequent years other institutions and dedi-

Head from a stone lintel at
Yaxchilán.

cated individuals joined in Maya research, and today there is an enormous mass of published material.

The modern archaeologist is a careful man, sifting dirt, paying attention to everything, noting everything, considering his material carefully, tentative about firm conclusions. He is aware that there are many possibilities for interpretation. He has much more factual material than his predecessors, but he is much more careful about generalizing from it.

Most archaeologists today agree that the Americas were originally populated by emigrants from Asia who came across a then-existing land bridge near the Bering Strait, although there is disagreement about when the earliest crossings were made. There is evidence of man in Middle America around 11,000 B.C., but possibly the earliest people came forty thousand years ago. Probably these were not large migrations, but movements of small bands of people.

But the acceptance of the Bering Strait migrations does not begin to answer all the questions. These people, of course, brought tools and techniques and cultural habits from their Old World homes, but did they for the most part develop their culture here? Were there possibly later migrations by boat across the Pacific that brought cultures more developed than those of the people who had wandered down the Pacific coast from Alaska to Mexico and Peru? If this is true, it would help to explain why the great civilizations of the New World were in Mesoamerica and Peru, remote from the Bering Strait, and with no trace of high cultures along the way.

In the first half of the twentieth century it was considered rash for a scholar to suggest that there might have been some transoceanic contact between the Old World and the Americas in ancient times. The reaction to the nineteenth-century romantics was strong. In recent years, however, the question of Far Eastern influence on the development of New World civilizations has been brought up frequently, backed by scholarly arguments. Whereas in the past, theorists were seeking the origins of the American Indians, the present argument is whether or not there was any contact between the cultures of Asia and existing cultures in the New World and, if so, how important such a contact might have been.

Evidence has been presented of possible contact around 3000 B.C. on the coast of Ecuador, where excavators found a culture with simple tools and sophisticated pottery. The pottery was manufactured by techniques similar to those existing in Japan at the same period or slightly earlier. Since this is some of the earliest pottery in the New World, it suggests an intrusive influence, possibly brought by a Japanese fishing boat that had been blown off its course. Equally ancient pottery, however, has been found on the Caribbean coast of Colombia and in Panama.

Given the antiquity of the traits of civilization in the Americas, it is hard to construct a reasonable theory which makes the origins of New World civilization dependent on transoceanic influences; but, given many similar traits, it is also hard to argue against the impossibility of at least occasional contact. However, definite proof is hard to come by.

Visual similarities between various Asian and New World objects have long been noted. A number of scholars have now made lists of cultural traits shared by the peoples of Asia and the New World during specific periods in history. Examples are bark paper, the parasol, the litter, the fan, the cylindrical tripod jar, the pottery mold, the serpent balustrade, and the interlace design in sculpture. The problem is whether these traits were developed independently or whether they were diffused by contact. A large list of shared traits would suggest that there may have been contact. A control requirement for such a list is that the trait in the donor country must antedate its appearance in the borrowing country.

Pottery from Asia and the New World is being compared for similarities in design and technique; studies of wind and water currents are being made to determine whether or not Asian boats might have drifted and been blown across the Pacific; and linguistic studies are being made to determine possible relationships between peoples. Although linguists do not admit the basic relationship of any Old World to any New World languages, these studies do indicate that some words may have been diffused from one language to another. When enough evidence of various kinds is put together, a good case may be made for pre-Columbian trans-pacific voyages.

Archaeology is like a jigsaw puzzle. In the archaeologist's laboratory there is a pile of potsherds—fragments of unpainted pottery lying in a heap—which have been dug up in an archaeological excavation and must be put together to form a pot again. However, there are no sky colors to match up, as in ordinary jigsaw puzzles, and there are no distinctive gerrymander shapes. Some pieces may be missing, or some edges may be broken so that pieces that actually belong together do not seem to fit. It is not even certain that all the fragments in the pile come from the same pot. Yet the archaeologist must put the pieces together to reconstruct the original shape.

A similar task faces him in reconstructing the whole of the past with which he deals. People have lived on the earth for thousands of years, leaving layer on layer of trash behind them—skeletons, buildings, sculpture, flints, fossilized food, thousands of complicated or simple things. Not only have they left objects, they have also left traditions, languages, ways of behaving. The archaeologist takes all the bits and pieces he knows about the people he is studying and tries to put them together to give a picture of how people lived, what they believed, how they behaved, what kind of world they inhabited, and what kinds of things they created.

Human beings have always been interested in worlds beyond their own. In the old days they could go off on voyages of discovery in sailing ships; in the present they seek new worlds in spacecraft. Archaeology is another kind of voyage of discovery—a journey into the past, not through the easy imaginings of a time machine, but by the hard work of putting together all the shreds of evidence that indicate what people were like in other ages. The puzzle the archaeologists are working out is a kind of detective story, one that does not have a single plot but is the story of how millions of people lived over a period of thousands of years. The puzzle is both vertical in time and horizontal in space.

The archaeologist literally digs for his facts. What he finds in greatest quantity are pieces of pottery. Potsherds, lowly and dull to the layman, can make an enormous contribution to the archaeologist's knowledge. Styles change in pottery as in everything else, and each level the archaeologist digs yields different kinds of pottery, which tell not only the story of the progressive occupation of a site, but also the relationship in time between different sites that have the same type of pottery. Some excavations have brought up pottery that comes from a different place entirely, indicating trade or some relationship between the two places. Pottery is valuable not only because it is plentiful, but because it is indestructible. Wood and cloth rot away, stone is eroded, but pottery, although it may break, endures.

The modern archaeologist, however, does not simply dig ruins and examine potsherds, although these are basic and important activities. Everything is grist to his mill. He examines other evidence with dozens of techniques and is helped by people trained in many other fields. Geologists add valuable information; for instance, samples of earth taken with a core drill can tell much about the sequence of human occupation of a site. Geological analyses of stone can indicate trade routes, for stone objects found in a particular site may have been carved from the stone of another area. Since flint comes from one part of the Maya area and obsidian from another, the distribution of artifacts made from these stones can indicate much about the nature of ancient trade. Botanists, too, contribute to archaeological studies. Not only can they tell what the former vegetation of a place was, but they can piece together much information from fossilized pollen, seeds, or remains of food. Many of the attempts to understand Maya ecology and to seek the causes of the fall of the Maya civilization have centered around agricultural and geological studies. Zoologists can reconstruct the past fauna of an area. Linguistic studies also contribute to knowledge of the past: the study of present-day language distribution tells something about the origins and relationships and movements of peoples in the past. Borrowed words in the Maya language are indicative of outside influences. The modern Maya languages are also useful in the attempts to read the ancient Maya hieroglyphs. Architects are often part of archaeological teams, helping in the study, reconstruction, and recording of ruins. Even medicine aids archaeology, as when physicians examine skeletons for signs of nutritional deficiency, seeking causes for the decline of the Maya. The art historian defines regional art styles and shows the development and spread of the influence of a particular group of people, for artistic influences often reflect political influences. The spread of art styles also adds to the understanding of trade relationships. One of the archaeologist's collaborators who appeals most to the imagination is the diver, who brings to the surface water-hidden

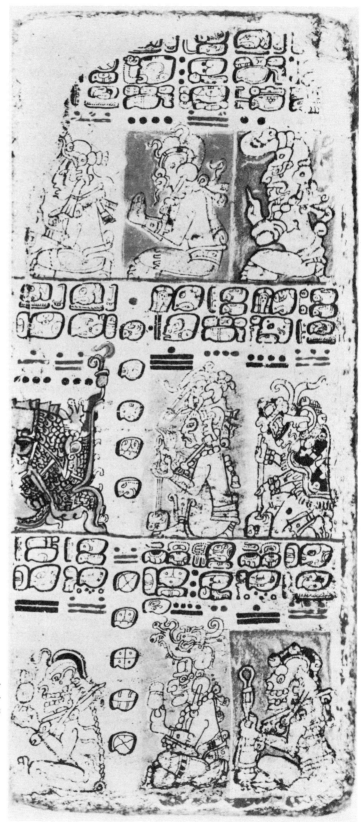

A page from the Dresden Codex, a pre-Conquest manuscript, showing Maya deities and hieroglyphic writing.

clues for the archaeologist's puzzle. The lakes and natural wells of the Maya area were used for offerings to water deities, and divers have found rich offerings of ancient objects in their depths.

Many modern tools and techniques help in the reconstruction of the past. Buried sculpture has been found with magnetometers. Computers are used for handling quantities of statistical data. Thermoluminescence testing—based on the light and glow emitted by a mineral when heated to 500° C.—can be used to date pottery, and neutron activation analysis or trace element analysis, using x-ray fluorescence, can be used to determine the sources of various materials; obsidian (volcanic glass), for example, can be analysed in this way. Obsidian can also be dated by hydration analysis, for, when freshly cut, it absorbs water to form hydration layers that can be measured by microscope. A broadly useful method for determining age is radiocarbon, or carbon 14, an isotope in all organic matter that decays immutably at a known rate. By measuring the percentage of carbon 14 surviving, materials such as textiles and charred wood can be dated. Space exploration, too, has aided archaeology, for aerial photography and other remote sensing techniques have helped in discovering and mapping sites and in the observation of geographical interrelationships. This world of new technology is a far cry from that of the dreamers of the lost continent of Atlantis.

Modern civilization has been both helpful and destructive. Many archaeological finds have been made while digging for roads or buildings. (The Leyden Plate, which was for a time the earliest known dated Maya object, was discovered a hundred years ago when a canal was being dug in Guatemala.) The area around Guatemala City has yielded an enormous amount of material during excavations for houses, roads, and pipes. The bulldozer has produced vast finds, not as the archaeologist would like them, lying in their proper layers, unbroken and intact, but nevertheless clues for his puzzle. One curiously influential factor in Maya archaeology has been the modern habit of chewing gum. The chicleros who go into the jungles to collect the sap from the sapodilla tree to obtain the raw material for chewing gum have frequently stumbled on Maya ruins (chicleros have been peripherally employed by archaeologists just for the purpose of reporting and leading them to ruins), and the trails and airstrips used for bringing out the sap, or chicle, have proved invaluable to the archaeologist. The airplane has opened up areas previously accessible only by the most difficult journeys; it has enabled supplies to be brought in and has made possible new working techniques.

However, it has also allowed smugglers to remove sculpture from the forest with great ease. Oil exploration in the heart of the Maya country has been another mixed blessing in the development of Maya archaeology.

In many cases modern civilization has made possible discoveries that might not otherwise have been made. On the other hand, the modern archaeologist is usually unhappy with the bulldozer that wrecks his site and clumsily fishes up precious relics of the past—a bulldozer in a pottery shop. He is unhappy with the grave robber, not so much because the grave robber spirits the object away to sell it on the souvenir or art market, but because he has removed a piece of the puzzle from its archaeological environment. The archaeologist will never know now exactly how or where the piece was found, because the grave robber, to protect himself, must keep his secret. Where things are found and what they are found with is just as important as what they are. When the site is destroyed, the record—which is what the site really is—is destroyed forever and the picture of the past will never be quite complete.

But despite the depredations of man and machinery, the archaeologist is constantly acquiring more and more pieces that fit together to solve the puzzling paradox of the life of the ancient Maya. Each year brings the excavation of more sites, the decipherment of more hieroglyphs, the interpretation of more material, and a clearer picture of the Maya world.

II.
THE PLACE AND THE PEOPLE

In the study of history and anthropology large supranational areas that are culturally related to each other can often be discerned. Among the pre-Columbian cultures, one such area is called Mesoamerica. Mesoamerica includes the lower half of Mexico, Guatemala, Belize (British Honduras), western Honduras, El Salvador, and a strip along the Pacific down through Nicaragua into Costa Rica. There were two great areas of pre-Columbian civilization in the New World: one in Mesoamerica, the other in the central Andes. The Maya area is part of Mesoamerica, a territory linked not only by communication and trade and a continuity of tradition and influence, but by shared cultural traits. The inhabitants of Mesoamerica before the Spanish Conquest had many things in common: large ceremonial and market centers with mounds or pyramids, stone public architecture and monumental stone sculpture, ball courts, impressive art styles in many media, books and maps, complex calendars and astronomical calculations, numerical notation systems, populations of relatively great size and density with a hierarchical social structure, a concentration of natural and human resources for public enterprise, extensive foreign trade, the same staple crops, ritual human sacrifice, and a number of other similar customs and kinds of objects.

Mesoamerica is a region of tremendous geographical variety. It includes temperate climate and tropical climate, highlands and lowlands, rain forests, and virtual desert. It is diverse in flora and fauna. In one small part of it there are more kinds of corn and more kinds of birds than exist in the entire United States. Its crops, its animals, and its mineral resources vary from place to place. This means not only a variety of materials to work with, but a natural setup for trading these materials. In spite of the difficulties of much of the terrain and the seeming isolation of many regions, and in spite of the independence of cultures, there is a long history of interrelationship and, in the period of its greatest development, a kind of cross-fertilization.

The Maya area, roughly a vertical rectangle on the map, is carved out of several countries—southern Mexico, most of Guatemala, all of Belize, and parts of Honduras and El Salvador. It is broken up into three zones that are distinct geographical and cultural divisions.

The Central Maya area is not only geographically central; it is also the section where the civilization reached its peak. It includes the Guatemalan Department of the Petén and adjacent parts of Guatemala, the neighboring parts of the states of Chiapas, Tabasco, and Campeche in Mexico, as well as all of Belize and part of Honduras. Around its southern rim this area is elevated, but its heart is lowland jungle. The Central Maya area consists largely of a tall, fast-growing tropical rain forest of Spanish cedars, giant ceibas (wild cotton trees), varieties of palm trees, mahogany, sapodilla and occasional rubber trees. Liana vines swing from the trees, and orchids grace the damp denseness of the jungle. It is an area difficult to cultivate, difficult to work in, difficult to move about in. There are few natural resources. There is no metal or igneous rock. Geologically it has a limestone foundation with thin soil. It is low, rolling country whose heavy forest is varied occasionally by rivers, lakes, swamps, and grassy savannas. An area that is not today a geographical unit or a political entity, it is at present almost uninhabited. At the peak of the ancient Maya civilization, however, it had a large, widespread population of seemingly peaceful peoples whose languages were essentially the same, who had a cultural unity, and who traded extensively.

The second geographical subdivision is the Northern Maya area, comprised of the Mexican state of Yucatán, and most of the states of Campeche and Quintana Roo—that is, the northern Yucatán peninsula. The tip of the peninsula is flat, rocky, and today prickly with sisal plantations. Sisal was probably grown here in ancient Maya times, as ropes made of the plant were used to move enormous blocks of stone for Maya buildings and sculpture. The only elevation in the area is in the southern part of the state of Yucatán, where the Puuc hills rise gently above the

flat ground. Bishop Landa described Yucatán in the sixteenth century as "the country with least earth that I have ever seen, since all of it is one living rock and has wonderfully little earth, so that there are few places where one can dig down six feet without striking great layers of very large rocks." Rock cairns are piled in the fields. Stone fences line the roads, and houses are often made of stone. Going northward from the Central area toward the coast at the tip of the peninsula, the land becomes dry, the rainfall decreases, and the vegetation is scrub growth. The limestone that underlies the soil is more porous than that of the Central area and lets the rain seep through to underground drainage. There are virtually no rivers and few lakes, but where the limestone crust has fallen in, there are places where water is stored naturally, the so-called cenotes, or wells, which furnish all the water this area has. Although the Northern area and the Central area are distinguishable in terms of culture and environment, they merge as parts of a single flat peninsula and are sometimes referred to together simply as the Maya Lowlands.

The third Maya subdivision, the Southern, or Highland, area, consists of the mountainous region of Guatemala and adjacent parts of El Salvador, as well as parts of Honduras on the west and Mexican Chiapas on the east. This region includes rugged volcanic ranges, high fertile valleys with a cool climate, plateaus fringed with oak and pine, and rolling, cypress-covered subtropical foothills. The rainfall is adequate, and the land is drained by swift rivers.

These areas are not only distinct geographically, but they are distinct in terms of Maya history. Although they were all occupied in very early times, there was a movement from one to the other in terms of cultural florescence: the Highland, or Southern, area probably gave the impetus to the development of Maya culture; the civilization developed to its highest peak in the Central area; and its last flash of glory took place in the Northern area.

Maya history is rooted in the dim past of Mesoamerica, where, twelve thousand years ago, people roamed this region in bands as hunters, killing small game with projectile points or trapping and snaring. Sometimes they gathered wild plant foods and then moved on as the plants became locally scarce. Their nomadic life did not permit them many possessions. They often lived temporarily in caves and rock shelters. Thin layers of trash indicate that they were not sedentary, and the vegetable remains in the trash tell what periods of the year the shelters

Ruins of a temple at Yaxchilán, showing the tropical rain forest growth.

were lived in. Occasionally they were inhabited for more than one season, but rarely longer. About nine thousand years ago there was a shift from a primary emphasis on hunting to a predominance of food gathering. Most of the plants collected were wild, but squash and avocado were domesticated about this time. The earliest fossil evidence for domesticated corn, found in a cave in southern Mexico, has been given a radiocarbon date indicating that it is about six thousand years old. Gradually more tools and utensils were developed: flaked projectile points for hunting, and stone tools for chipping and scraping, chopping and grinding. Gourds were used for dishes. Some tools were made of bones and sticks. Cactuslike plants were cut into strands and woven into bags, nets, kilts, mats, and baskets. The burials of these early people seem to be curiously elaborate, with a quantity of burial goods and a suggestion of cannibalism. The ritualistic society of the Classic period is perhaps very deep-rooted.

The first signs of village life occur around 3500 B.C. By 1500 B.C. some of the roaming bands of hunters and gatherers had settled into a sedentary life. The period from 1500 B.C. to A.D. 300 is called the Pre-Classic period. People had now developed agriculture to a point where they had to live in villages in order to tend their crops. They built houses and made more useful and complicated kinds of objects than they could have as nomads. They began to make pottery. More plants were domesticated, and those that had been domesticated earlier were improved. In time they began to build ceremonial centers, and started constructing mounds on which to put their important buildings, which must have been religious structures.

The outstanding people from the Pre-Classic period were the Olmec, who lived from about 1200 until about 300 B.C. on the east coast of Mexico in the states of Tabasco and southern Veracruz. The influence—and perhaps the actual domination—of the Olmec was felt over a much wider area. The Olmec were a remarkable people who established a pattern for much of later Mexican culture. We do not know who they were or where they came from. It has been suggested that they were outsiders, perhaps even a small group of immigrants from across the Pacific. But they clearly had roots with earlier peoples and relationships with the agriculturalists who then inhabited most of Mesoamerica. The Olmec obviously developed a surplus-producing economy, allowing them to maintain skillful artists, traders, and an elite priestly group. They apparently had a stratified, ritualistic society like that of the Maya.

Olmec colossal stone head.

They built ceremonial centers with mounds and made monumental sculpture. The beginnings of hieroglyphic writing are probably creditable to the Olmec, for Olmec art consists of a number of glyphlike symbols or motifs used interchangeably. Most of these derive from nature, particularly from the characteristics of reptiles, raptorial birds, and the jaguar.

These themes—especially that of the jaguar—haunt not only Olmec sculpture and pottery, but recur throughout Mesoamerican art and thought. The Maya word for jaguar also means "sorcerer." Maya chieftains often had "Jaguar" as a part of their names; the first men in the Quiché Maya creation myth were named after the jaguar. Important people wore jaguar skins, and the sacred objects and thrones of chieftains were covered with them. Jaguar jaws have been found in Maya graves. Even contemporary Indians endow the jaguar with supernatural power in legend and myth.

Today a traveler in the forests of Mexico or Guatemala, moving under the mahogany and sapodilla trees, is aware that jaguars are there. They come out only at night and stay away from people, and yet they make their presence felt. Their deep, hoarse cries can be heard after dark. A North American, with no heritage of a jaguar legend, still instinctively reacts to the mystique of the big cat that prowls like a heavily built leopard. The Indians who inhabit this area today all have stories to tell about the jaguar, although they may never have seen one. The Indians who dwelled in the forest in ancient times must have felt even more strongly the magic of its presence. The largest cats in the New World, jaguars are, like man, hunters and eaters of meat, so man wanted to identify with their power. The jaguar was associated not only with the waterways along which it hunted and fished, but also with caves, with the heart of the earth, and, hence, with crops and fertility. Because it is a rain-forest creature, the jaguar is associated with rain in the drier areas of Mesoamerica.

Although there are no verbal legends from the Olmec people, their sculpture shows that they may have had a myth in which a woman mated with a jaguar. Olmec art is full of creatures who are part human and part feline, with flattened noses and snarling mouths and fangs. Sometimes they are more human, sometimes more jaguar; often they are a combination of human infant and jaguar, and are called "were-jaguars." There must have been a number of kinds or forms of were-jaguars.

The Olmec culture, unlike that of the Maya, which has been known since the Spaniards arrived, was not identified until quite recently. About

Olmec jadeite axe with a were-jaguar face. Eleven inches high.

a hundred years ago colossal human heads of stone, six to nine feet tall, were found in the forests of southern coastal Veracruz. These heads, flat-nosed, thick-lipped, helmeted, looking like football players, have been found in four sites. Monumental stelae (vertical blocks of stone) and massive "altars" were also found, as were small objects finely carved from jade and serpentine. When the first Olmec sculpture was discovered, many experts assumed that it was an aberrant form of Maya art, but gradually it was realized that this was an art style previously unknown. Some archaeologists thought that it was very early, whereas others believed that an art so advanced must fall within the great period in Meso-america, A.D. 300 to 900.

Knowledge is constantly changing. Recent investigations of a possibly pre-Olmec site in Belize, which has Maya building characteristics, may once again upset the current thinking about sequences and influences.

The Late Pre-Classic and Proto-Classic periods—the time between the Olmec culture and that of the Maya—lasted from about 300 B.C. to A.D. 300. This era was characterized by a Post-Olmec art style that was spread from Veracruz across Central Mexico and down to the Pacific slopes of southern Mexico and Guatemala, mingling Olmec elements with new visual ideas. The art style called Izapan, after the site of Izapa in Chiapas, at the very southeastern tip of Mexico, belonged to this spread and was probably the most important transitional style between that of the Olmec and that of the Maya. The types of objects and styles of art found at Izapan sites relate to both Olmec and Maya artifacts. Scholars now believe that many inventions previously credited to the Maya were actually initiated in this Late Pre-Classic period. The Long Count system of noting time, later used on Maya monuments, is first shown on an Izapan monument at Chiapa de Corzo (Chiapas) and on a post-Olmec monument in the Olmec part of Veracruz. The bar-and-dot system of counting, which will be discussed later, was probably invented in the central Mexican state of Oaxaca at this time.

Many of the Maya sites were inhabited in Pre-Classic times. Maize pollen dating back as far as 800 B.C. has been found in the Maya area. Recent work by the University of Pennsylvania at Tikal, the great Maya city in the Petén, shows that people were living there at least as long ago as 600 B.C. By the Late Pre-Classic period, Tikal was apparently much the same in terms of physical site plan as it was in its later heyday. The Maya area generally seems to have had a considerable population by Late Pre-Classic times, and in this period it began to gather momentum for its culminating development. The beginnings of stone architecture at Tikal date from around 200 B.C.; there is evidence of monumental sculpture from about 100 B.C., and traces of paintings with glyphs exist from the first century B.C.

Although there was Late Pre-Classic settlement in the Central area, this was a more impressive period in the Highlands. Kaminaljuyú, on the outskirts of Guatemala City, was a large, important ceremonial center whose art was closely related to that of the Izapan sites, which were also of considerable importance. Stelae, the carved vertical shafts of stone that are a typical form of Maya sculpture, were erected at this time in these sites, and in Oaxaca as well. Late Pre-Classic and Early Classic sites existed as far away as Salvador, where recently discovered evidence of volcanic eruption around A.D. 250 or 300 has been cited as a possible cause of the movement of the Maya away from this area. The Early Classic development in the Central area was, however, well under way by this time.

The greatest period of the Maya came in the years between A.D. 300 and 900, the Classic period. To speak of a Classic period recalls ancient Greece and Rome, and indeed the Classic period of the Maya was a golden age, a time of intellectual ferment, creative activity, the building of outstanding public architecture, the carving of sculpture, the elaborate recording of texts. There were advances in mathematics, astronomy, and writing. The development of art and knowledge went along with the development of a complex and stratified urban society clustered around ceremonial centers.

The Classic period was not only a great period in the Maya area, but all over Mesoamerica. In central Veracruz an important culture thrived, with handsome architecture and sculpture. In the Valley of Mexico the influential city of Teotihuacán flourished; Monte Albán in Oaxaca was the impressive center of a Zapotec-speaking people. The Classic cultures shared a common high cultural level and they profited from being part of a large community of ideas and techniques. Communication between them was important. Teotihuacán-style pottery has been found in the Maya area, and one of the finest Maya jades is reported to have been found at Teotihuacán. Yet these cultures remained distinct in terms of art styles, ideologies, and social structures.

Most of the achievements of the Classic period were presaged in the Pre-Classic, but there is no one region in Mesoamerica where all the Classic accomplishments were foreshadowed. Different places specialized in different things. The Classic period did not develop, that is, in one region because in the Pre-Classic this region had produced good pottery, or in another because in the late Pre-Classic this region had carved monumental stone sculpture. It was variety and interaction that gave the Classic period stimulus and richness, and created intellectual and aesthetic ferment.

In the impressive achievements of Classic Mesoamerica, however, there are curious lacunae. For example, the wheel was never used anywhere in the New World. There were no wheeled carts; there was no potter's wheel. There are objects that were probably road rollers, but the wheel was evidently not used for transportation. Wheeled toys, found in many parts of Mexico, are the only known examples of the use of the wheel in the Americas before the Spanish arrived at the beginning of the sixteenth century. There is an interesting parallel in the fact that the Egyptians did not have the wheel during their great pyramid-building period. It was invented in the Old World probably five thousand years ago. Migrations into the New World began before the invention of the wheel, but it seems odd that later arrivals did not utilize it or that, if there were later transpacific contacts, it was not introduced into the New World by the people who made the contacts.

When important inventions are not made, one begins to look for reasons why. In much of the New World the wheel would not have been useful. In Peru, for example, the mountainous terrain was not practical for wheel-bearing roads, as it was too difficult going uphill and too fast going down. The Old World certainly provided conditions more conducive to the invention of the wheel than the New World jungle of the Maya. Most of the great Classic Maya ceremonial centers were in the tropical rain forest, and even in the middle of the twentieth century, roads—where there are roads—in this area are impassable because of mud most of the year. A modern road map of the Maya area shows the virtual uselessness of the wheeled vehicles today; there are no roads to speak of. One must fly or go by boat into most of the Lowland Maya sites. Even in the dry season, planes cannot always land on jungle airstrips—where airstrips have been cleared—because of the mud, and the jungle growth is constantly encroaching on cleared areas. In this area the wheel is sometimes more trouble than it is help. It is true that the Maya built roads, but they were used for processions on foot rather than for wheeled traffic. The wheel could have been used in some parts of the New World—the valley floors of Mexico, for example. But there is another and perhaps more important reason for this failure of invention. The New World lacked draft animals. In neither Mexico nor Peru were there horses, oxen, donkeys, or any other animals that were domesticable and strong enough to pull carts along roads.

Another invention missing in Classic Mesoamerica was metalworking. In the Old World ages are named by the metals people had learned to work, such as the Bronze Age and the Iron Age. Metalworking is a criterion of the progress of civilization. In the New World gold was worked in South America two thousand years before the Spanish Conquest, but in Mesoamerica metal was not worked until about A.D. 1000. The great Classic Maya civilization was a Stone Age culture, using stone tools, flint points, and obsidian blades. Again, there is a practical reason for this failure to invent: no notable metal deposits have been found in the Maya area.

The accomplishments of Mesoamerica in general and the Maya in particular are nevertheless impressive, and the Classic period produced one of the great civilzations of its time.

PHOTOGRAPH COURTESY OF THE DUMBARTON OAKS COLLECTIONS

Izapan-style incising on a pectoral, showing a seated figure and a hieroglyphic text. Ten and a half inches long.

Change is rarely abrupt. Our age has the fastest rate of acceleration in history, but in the past changes took place very slowly over millennia. The transition from hunting to agriculture was slow. The development of a complex urban society was slow. Although well-established trade routes are a criterion of high civilization in the New World, it is apparent that there were trade routes even in Pre-Classic times. The Olmec, on the east coast of Mexico, surely traded across Mexico, and probably along a route which led them as far as Costa Rica. As the population increased and the relationships between villages became stronger, villages undoubtedly shared ceremonial occasions and traded with each other, forming the basis for the highly developed community and ceremonial life of Classic times. As urbanization and centralization developed and populations grew, agriculture became more organized and depended more on trade to support the population. Because this change was slow and subtle, there was no abrupt beginning of the Classic period.

Yet there are criteria that clearly mark the beginning of the Classic period in the Central Maya area. The use of the corbel vault in building construction (beginning about A.D. 250), the manufacture of polychrome pottery (also dating from about A.D. 250), and the carving of dated monuments (the earliest dated stela thus far found—at Tikal—has a date of A.D. 292) are the touchstones of the Classic civilization. By A.D. 300 the Classic period was well under way. There are two divisions of the period: the phase from about A.D. 300 to 550—the Early Classic—and the Late Classic, from about A.D. 550 to 900. The Late Classic is marked by changes in architectural construction, in sculpture styles, and in pottery.

For six hundred years the Central Maya civilization thrived, and then, about A.D. 900, the great Central ceremonial centers became quiet. The reason is not known. The sites were not all absolutely abandoned, of course. People did not totally vanish into the forest; some of them continued to live in villages around the centers. But there was a severe decrease in population, and the cities were no longer important centers. The priests and nobles were gone and the rigid social structure had broken down. Sometimes people lived in the former "palaces" and temples, cooking outside the buildings and throwing away trash wherever it was convenient. Although there is pottery from this period, no new dated monuments were carved, and few buildings were built. The people who lingered in and around these cities for about a century after the last dated monuments were probably Maya, a dwindling population eking out an existence in cities that were falling into ruins.

Unlike the Central Maya sites, the Northern area was inhabited long after the forest cities had been abandoned. It was once thought that the Maya moved from the Central area to Yucatán at the end of the Classic period, and for a long time the terms "Old Empire" and "New Empire" were in use. However, recent excavations have proved that many of the "New Empire" sites were actually occupied in very early times. Dzibilchaltún, on the tip of the Yucatán peninsula, was occupied continuously for perhaps as long as four thousand years, from the Pre-Classic through the Post-Classic. Dzibilchaltún, where the National Geographic Society and Tulane University have recently been working, was one of the largest cities in Mesoamerica and one of the very few which was continuously occupied.

Descendants of the ancient Maya still live in their old territory. They have mingled with other Indians and with Spanish stock, but, as much as they can in a modern world, they persist in their old traditions and many of them still speak Maya. The twentieth-century visitor to Yucatán can purchase a little English-Spanish-Maya dictionary and is encouraged to pick up a few words of Maya. There are now about fifteen Maya languages spoken, which are divided into two major groups—Highland and Lowland. Dictionaries of these now being compiled are helpful to scholars in the decipherment of Maya hieroglyphs.

The Maya people are short and sturdily built, with broad heads, Roman noses, and somewhat receding jaws. Sometimes in the Petén one sees a face that is almost exactly like that on a Classic relief carving. Yet there are differences; the modern Maya does not perpetuate his ancestor's artificially induced marks of beauty and distinction. Crossed eyes were achieved in ancient times by a bead or a small disc of wood dangled from a child's hair in front of the eyes. As recently as a hundred years ago, John Lloyd Stephens found a number of "squinty eyes" in Yucatán. The septum of the nose was drilled so that a nose ornament could be worn. The ears were not merely pierced, but had a hole in the lobe through which an ornament as wide as an inch in diameter could be fitted. Teeth were filed to a point or inlaid with decorations of iron pyrites or jade. Another convention was the deformation of the skull; the head was flattened in infancy by the pressure of two slightly concave pieces of wood. Bishop Landa describes this process in the sixteenth century, but sculpture shows that the practice dates back at least as far as Olmec times. Hair—even the men's—was worn long. "On top they burned a space like a great tonsure," Landa writes, "and thus the hair grew long below, while that of the top of the head was left short. And they braided it and made a wreath of it around their heads, leaving the queue behind like tassels." Classic-period sculpture shows the hair intricately dressed in complicated headgear.

Bodies were tattooed, as Landa described: "The more they do this, the more brave and valiant are they considered, as tattooing is accompanied by great suffering, and is done in this way. Those who do the work first paint the part which they wish with color and afterwards they delicately cut in the paintings, and so with the blood and coloring matter the marks remained in the body. This work is done a little at a time on account of the extreme pain."

Landa reports that "their clothing was a band of the width of a hand, which served them for drawers and breeches. They wound it several times around the waist, so that one end fell in front and one end behind, and these ends the women made with a great deal of care and with feather-work. And they wore large square mantles and tied them over their shoulders. They wore sandals of hemp or of the dry untanned skin of the deer, and they wore no other garments." The nobles also wore a sleeveless jacket, and their sandals and mantles were more elaborate. They wore bracelets, necklaces and sometimes pendants of shell or jade.

Landa also writes: "All the men used mirrors. . . . They bathed frequently. . . . They were great lovers of perfumes, and for this they used bouquets of flowers and odoriferous herbs, arranged with great care. They had the custom of painting their faces and bodies red, and, although it was very unbecoming to them, yet they thought it very pleasing."

The scale of the building projects in the ancient ceremonial centers testifies to an organized, orderly society with large labor resources. Farming and trade must also have been well organized. Landa writes that the Yucatecans "have the good habit of helping each other in all their labors. At the time of sowing those who do not have their own people to do their work, join together in groups of twenty, more or less, and all together they do the work of all of them." He also states that when making a visit the visitor presented the host with a gift and the host gave another gift in return. The modern Maya are sociable; they like to work together; they have strong family bonds; and they are hospitable, considerate, and polite. But the Maya today has little inclination for leadership. He is perhaps more the descendant of the peasant farmer than of the noble and priestly class who ruled Classic Maya society. Sadly, he seems to have lost the great artistic gift of his ancestors.

In former times the Maya believed that certain days in their calendar were fortunate and certain days were evil; the modern Maya considers Tuesdays and Fridays unlucky, Mondays and Saturdays lucky. The ancient Maya lived in a society in which religious ceremony was woven into daily life. The present-day Maya tends to be fatalistic and superstitious. Most of the modern Maya are nominal Christians, although they still preserve pre-Christian practices. The Lacandon, a diminishing branch of the Maya who live in the forests near the Usumacinta River, have never been converted. Many of them wear long hair and long garments, and it is still possible to find the offerings of copal made in their pilgrimages to the great Maya ruins of Yaxchilán and Bonampak. Some of them come into the city of Mérida to sell their bows and arrows and jewelry to tourists, looking like creatures from another age.

The Maya have survived many influences and invasions, but the encroachment of the modern world threatens to destroy forever the vestiges of their ancient civilization.

Sir Eric S. Thompson, Maya archaeologist, with Lacandon men at Bonampak.

PHOTOGRAPH COURTESY OF GILES G. HEALEY

III.
THE CITIES

The Department of the Petén in Guatemala is the heart of the Central Maya area. This is a vast sea of jungle broken occasionally by a river or a grassy stretch of savanna. As one flies over it, one sees no towns and only rarely a village. The landscape is dense and green. And then, on the horizon, white masonry looms above the jungle like the crests of waves on the sea. These are the ruins of the ancient temples of Tikal, a Classic Maya city built on a slight rise in the gently rolling country. The plane lands on an airstrip cut from the jungle and the passengers walk along the dirt—or mud—road used by the jeeps and trucks of the archaeologists working on the site. The vegetation is rank. There are tall trees with strangely sculptural trunks, and the leaves of the plants are often red and green. There are parrots and vivid toucans; there may also be a familiar North American catbird wintering in the South. Suddenly there looms ahead a temple on its pyramid, a spectral presence overgrown with trees and vines. The main part of the site lies just beyond. Here, in the silence of the jungle, two temples on tall pyramids face each other across a large plaza, surrounded by complexes of buildings and other pyramids and lined along one side with a row of stelae and altars.

What is now seen at Tikal, which means "Place of Voices," is a pale ghost image of what was once there, a magnificent city of handsomely decorated buildings and sculpture, now largely destroyed by time and vegetation. Other, little-explored sites may have been as large, but Tikal seems to be the greatest of the Central Lowland Maya cities, its main precinct covering about a square mile, the suburbs extending for two or three miles around it. The University of Pennsylvania worked there for twelve years, but the site is so vast that only parts of it were cleared, excavated, and consolidated. In any other field but archaeology, one might say that the surface had only been scratched, yet the work here is extensive compared with that at other cities in this area.

Although there has been much argument on the subject, it has generally been thought that Maya cities in the Central area were not true urban concentrations. In the Highland area, Kaminaljuyú was a large ceremonial and residential center as far back as Middle Pre-Classic times, and in Yucatán, in the Post-Classic period, Mayapán was a residential city. The cities of the Central area were sacred centers—monuments to the power of god-kings—and they were also centers of trade and secular activity. A small, select population lived in these sites permanently, but evidence for large-scale habitation is elusive.

There is great variation in population estimates, which are based on studies of house mounds and possible habitations, as well as on calculations of the labor force needed to construct and maintain a city and of the agricultural potential to support it. However, there is general agreement that the Central Maya area was one of the most densely populated regions in the pre-industrial world. An estimate of ten thousand people has been given for the six square miles of Tikal. The average population for the whole area may have been two hundred people per square mile. Archaeological evidence shows that the population was fairly well distributed over the entire countryside. House clusters in groups of five to twelve were surrounded by farming areas, and, for every fifty to a hundred house clusters, there was a small ceremonial center. The major ceremonial centers included several of these zones.

Maya society was surely a complex structure, with divine kings at the top. There must have been an aristocracy of civic-religious-military leaders, classes of artisans and merchants, peasant farmers, and those who were construction workers or servants. It appears to have been a strongly stratified society. Bishop Landa wrote that in the sixteenth century there were ruling families and that the people paid great respect to their chiefs and to the priests, who were also greatly respected by the lords. Only the priests and the lords knew the art of writing, and Landa got most of his information from a son of one of the chieftains who knew

The Great Plaza at Tikal, the heart of the ceremonial center, with Temple I in the background, a row of stelae and altars below, and the Central Acropolis to the left.

the Maya written language. The priests taught writing, astronomy, calendrics, and divination—all the esoteric lore of the Maya—to the sons of other priests and the sons of the lords.

The archaeological evidence from the Classic period certainly suggests high social status for some individuals. There were elaborate burials with rich grave goods, and the dead were sometimes accompanied by other people who were apparently committed to following the deceased into the afterlife. There are portrait representations in Classic art, and the hieroglyphic texts on sculpture contain biographical and commemorative material. Recent work on glyph decipherment has revealed the written names of cities, of kings, of ancestors (real and mythical), as well as words for "accession," "birth," and "death." The Late Classic period especially, with its handsome architecture and sculpture, and its profusion of skillfully made art objects, indicates a society whose priestly and noble class could command a large labor force to carry out its enterprises. The complicated intellectual knowledge and its apparently exclusive use by the upper classes further confirms this.

It may have been possible, however, for a member of the peasant class to rise in the structure. Recent studies of ancient settlement patterns —that is, the archaeological evidence of house mounds—as well as anthropological evidence from contemporary peoples who have been relatively untouched by modern civilization suggest that the society may not have been so stratified as the centers indicate. A number of house mounds have been recently excavated, and the skill of their construction and the quality of the objects found in them suggests that the people generally shared in the rich cultural level of the period. Moreover, the larger house mounds, which must have been the houses of the nobles, seem to be spread throughout the countryside rather than being concentrated in suburbs outside the ceremonial centers as it was once thought.

As for the anthropological evidence, there are communities in Highland Chiapas today which, although Christianized to some extent, seem to perpetuate a fairly ancient pattern and may shed light on Classic Maya social structure. In these communities there is a system of graded ranks in the population. Farmers come into the center periodically to serve in priestly offices, and each time it is at least possible for them to advance to a higher position in the system. They live temporarily in the civic and religious center, although only a small population lives there permanently. This social system seems to relate to ancient patterns and is possibly a survival of a Classic Maya way of life that would suggest greater society mobility than has been thought heretofore.

The exact social function of the ceremonial centers is still not clear, nor is the relationship of the ceremonial centers to the surrounding areas that sustained them. Another point that is still hazy is the political relationship of the centers to each other. How was power distributed or concentrated? Were there city-states? Can one speak of an "empire"? Was there a confederation or confederations? Some sites were certainly much more important than others, and a site hierarchy must have existed. Did a center like Tikal have power over all smaller sites, or was it one of four possible power-sharing centers, each with a cluster of lesser sites around it, which, in turn, would have their own satellites? Various patterns have been suggested, based on geography, on economic data, on house-mound surveys, on the size and distribution of sites, as well as on the texts on monuments, which seem to reveal something about an order or interrelationship of sites as well as marriage alliances and the possible conquering of other sites.

The Maya ceremonial center was laid out around a central plaza, and its buildings were usually oriented to the cardinal points of the compass. Maya houses tended to face on a courtyard, and the concept of the ceremonial plaza may well have grown up from the humbler courtyard. The plaza is flanked on all sides by terraces, platforms, pyramids, temples, and palaces. Of all the remnants of the vanished Maya, the most awesomely impressive are these architectural ruins. The buildings of the Petén and of Yucatán were built of limestone. Certain other Maya cities used distinctive local stone. The buildings of Copán, on the far eastern border of the Maya area, for example, were constructed of a tuff, which, when freshly cut, is a pale green like pistachio ice cream; it ages to gray with a pinkish overtone. Comalcalco, in the far western part of the Maya area, where there is no easily available building stone, has buildings made of brick. But limestone was the common material, and a number of limestone quarries have been found in and around the ceremonial centers. The rock surrounding the desired block of stone was cut away with stone tools, and the piece was then undercut and pried out of the quarry with wooden poles or wedges.

By Late Pre-Classic times the Maya were using limestone for their buildings and were burning lime to make mortar, as Maya construction relied heavily on the use of mortar. Limestone was burned on a huge cylindrical pile of wood, which took skill to construct so that there was complete combustion of the stone and wood without adding impurities to the resulting lime. It is remarkable that, considering the Stone Age tools

The Acropolis at Copán, a great Classic Maya center.

used for felling and moving the wood, the Maya produced sufficient mortar for their large number of buildings. Lime was used not only for great quantities of mortar but for plaster for the decoration of buildings (surfaces of buildings, as well as floors and stairways, were frequently covered with plaster), as a ground for mural paintings, and for stucco sculpture. Sometimes sacsab, a soft marl often found beneath the surface crust of limestone, was used as an aggregate for mortar.

Maya accomplishments are remarkable, and it is even more remarkable that they were accomplished with the simplest possible tools. Little work has been done on the study of Maya implements, and one cannot always be sure of the exact use of the tools that have been found, but

certainly the list is short. Stone tools were made of flint (which occurs
frequently in the Lowland limestone), obsidian and granite (imported
from the Highlands), limestone, and quartzite. The stone was fractured
with heavy weights or split with wedges, and then it was probably crum-
bled with pounding tools, or hammerstones, to prepare it for masonry
blocks. Then it was pecked, chipped, flaked, or abraded to achieve the
final surface. One of the implements most often found is a flint core that
has been percussion-flaked to make what must have been a general utility
tool used in masonry work and perhaps especially in the dressing of
stone. Celt-shaped stones may have been hafted for use as axes or used
as chisels or gouges. There were flint and obsidian tools for scraping,
polishing, and smoothing plaster. A few such tools have been found
made of pumice. Blades of flint and obsidian may have doubled as
knives and scraping tools, and some may have served as lance heads
rather than, or as well as, working tools. Some implements, because of
their shape and the way they are worn, seem to have been drills. There
were awls made of deer bones and some implements made of wood. The
Maya architect apparently had a plumb bob, but no level and no square.
And, of course, the only power he had was manpower. The stones of
Classic Maya buildings were well cut, dressed, and fitted. That the Maya
raised great buildings, decorated with skillfully made and elegant sculpture, was indeed a feat.

In looking at a Maya site, one is struck first by the truncated pyramids. Maya pyramids, unlike those of the Egyptians, are always flat-
topped, are usually stepped, and often supported buildings on their
summits. The tallest pyramids in the Maya area are those at Tikal, constructed in the late Classic period. The best known and best restored of
these is Temple I; the temple and the pyramid together are 145 feet high.
Temple IV, the most impressive temple in the Maya area, is 212 feet
high. Only partially restored now, it took an architect working with the
University of Pennsylvania expedition nine months to record this building
in drawings.

The concept of man-made mountains haunts our view of Mesoamerican architecture. The pyramids in the mountainous regions of Mexico and Guatemala seem to be reflections of the shapes of the mountains
that rim the horizon. In the Central Maya area there are no mountains
that would have directly inspired the Maya, and if the theory that the
Highland Maya gave the impetus to the great Classic development in
the Central area is correct, then perhaps the idea of pyramids came from

the Highland area. Even the Olmec, however, more than a millennium before, were erecting pyramids of impressive height. The idea of high sacred places is certainly almost universal.

The temples on top of the pyramids were both religious structures and monuments to Maya kings. The temples of Palenque contain sculpture reliefs of kings and deities, surrounded by symbolic paraphernalia, as well as texts which proclaim the historical and mythical lineage of Palenque kings. Important people were buried in temple floors; caches of precious objects lie beneath pavements; traces of ceremonial fires mar the surfaces. Ritual human sacrifice may have been performed in front of the temple, at the top of the long, impressive flight of steps.

The best-known early Maya pyramid is a small masonry structure at Uaxactún dating from the Late Pre-Classic period, a ceremonial platform that did not support a building. As time went on, pyramids tended to become higher, and increasingly elaborate temples were placed on them. There was a progression from fairly low platforms to the tall pyramids of the important centers in the Late Classic period, which were made of rubble and faced with cut stone. Staircases usually projected from the side of the pyramids, and the temples on top of them were one story. In some of the earlier or poorer centers the buildings were made of wattle and daub, or some other perishable material, with roofs made of thatch supported by poles at the corners. Temples at important centers in the Classic period were usually made of limestone and were set on a small raised platform on top of the pyramid. The temple might have had a painted plaster façade (like the Greeks, the Maya painted their buildings and sculpture, enhancing the drama of their religious centers) and an elaborate masonry roof.

The temples had from one to three rooms. Sometimes they were placed one behind the other, with a step up from each one to the next. When the walls were constructed to the desired height, the corbel-vaulted roof, a primary characteristic of Maya architecture in the Classic period, was formed by putting one stone on top of another, so that the upper stone projected past the lower one. The sequence of stones progressed farther and farther into the room so that finally the distance between the two sides could be bridged by a single slab of stone. The weight of these vaults presented construction problems, for mortar that had not dried properly might slip under the weight of the stone. Sometimes the builders let the mortar set before they proceeded, and sometimes they used wooden crossbeams to help hold the sides of the vault in

The Hieroglyphic Stairway at Copán. Late Classic period.

place; in a few sites they used stone crossbeams. Because of the need to support the vault of the ceiling, the rooms tended to be narrow and the walls thick and windowless. The Classic Maya architect, however, was always more concerned with the outer appearance of his buildings than with their inner space, although the Late Classic architect, having become more experienced and skillful, was able to construct lighter walls with a vault that spanned a larger space. The roofs frequently supported roof combs, rectangular elements as tall or taller than the building itself

Late Pre-Classic ceremonial platform with carved mask decoration, at Uaxactún.

PHOTOGRAPH COURTESY OF THE PEABODY MUSEUM, HARVARD UNIVERSITY

The interior of a building at Uxmal, showing the construction of the corbel vault.

and heavily decorated with sculpture. Some were hollow, like an A-frame over the roofs; some were solid, and sometimes they were perforated with windowlike openings.

Early Classic buildings, constructed between about A.D. 300 and 550, were typically built of large-tenoned stones deeply set in mortar. Late Classic architects tended to use a veneer masonry with shallow facing stones over a concrete made of mortar and rough lumps of limestones. Early Classic buildings sometimes had the slope of the vault beginning almost at the floor; later the vault began much farther up. The corbel

Part of a building at Labná, showing sculpture decoration and construction of arch and doorways.

PHOTOGRAPH COURTESY OF THE PEABODY MUSEUM, HARVARD UNIVERSITY

vault is typical of the Maya Lowlands in the Classic period; it was not
used in Highland Maya buildings, and it rarely appears in Northern-area
buildings constructed after the Classic period.

Most of the pyramids and temples were not built at one time.
Throughout the Maya area it was customary to build a newer and larger
pyramid over the old one, so that the old one became a core with the skin
of the new pyramid wrapped around it. Instead of tearing the old structure down completely, Maya builders covered it up with a new building.
In many sites, archaeologists have left the sightseer a glimpse of the
previous construction, or constructions, within the newer one.

The pyramids and the temples on top of them did not make up all
the major architecture of a Maya city. Equally impressive are grandiose
large buildings, often only slightly raised from the ground, some of which
are very complicated and have a large number of rooms. Often they are
built on several levels. True storied buildings are rare; the effect of many
stories was usually achieved by setting the upper rooms back so that they
rested on solid masonry. As with the pyramids and temples, new parts
were built over and around the old. These buildings, which were various
in size and arrangement, are usually called "palaces," although their function is a mystery. It has been suggested that they were used for meetings
or ceremonies, or perhaps as the temporary residences of priests and
sacrificial victims during ritual occasions—this was suggested by excavations at Uaxactún—or that they were, indeed, the palaces of royal families, uncomfortable as they may seem to modern observers. Stone benches,
which appear in many of these structures, have been cited as evidence
of possible habitation use. Plumbing arrangements have been found in
some buildings, as well as what may have been stoves or fireplaces. These
palaces are often known by names given them by the Spaniards, which
tell more about the Spaniards than about their actual pre-Hispanic use.
At Uxmal, for example, a building with numerous rooms surrounding a
courtyard is called "the Nunnery." Another particularly handsome building there has been named "the Governor's Palace." Although this latter
name is appropriate to the splendor of the architecture, it may have little
to do with its functional use. These palaces, like the temples, also contained caches and impressive burials.

There were other buildings in Classic Maya sites that give some
indication of the activities of the people. An important feature of Mesoamerican ceremonial centers was the ball court. Rubber is, of course,
indigenous to the jungles of this area, and heavy, solid balls of springy

rubber were used in games that must have been important ceremonial occasions all over Mesoamerica. The ball court was almost always placed near the center of the site. Some of the larger cities had as many as ten or fifteen ball courts. The Maya ball court was a long, narrow paved alley about 25 feet wide and 75 feet long, with a low masonry wall, or bench, along each side, and a sloping or vertical wall behind it, sometimes with sculptured reliefs. Carved stone markers were set in the floor and the walls of the court. The earliest formal ball court thus far known is an Early Classic one at Cópan, dating from about A.D. 300. The game must have existed for some time before that, however, for there are Middle Pre-Classic figurines that depict ball players. The Highland Maya ball courts are sometimes completely enclosed, unlike the open-ended ones of the Lowland Maya.

When the Spaniards came to the West Indies at the end of the fifteenth century, they found the Indians playing a game with a solid

Part of "the Nunnery," a palace at Uxmal, with pyramid and temple in the background.

rubber ball about six inches in diameter. Columbus took one of these
balls back to Europe, where rubber was as yet unknown. In 1528 Cortés
saw the ball game in Mexico.

The game was a combination of modern basketball, volley ball, soc-
cer, and jai alai. It was played by two teams of from two to eleven men
each. The ball measured from two to ten inches in diameter and weighed
an average of about five pounds. It was kept in motion by being hit with
the hips, thighs, forearms, and possibly the shoulders and heads of the
players, but not with their hands, feet, or calves. The ball could be
bounced against the side wall of the court. A score was made by striking
the side markers or forcing the ball into the opponents' end zone. A team
also scored if the ball went dead in the opponents' side of the court. Post-
Classic Maya ball courts—for example, at Chichén Itzá—had rings
through which the ball had to go instead of striking the marker. This was
apparently an influence from central Mexico.

A ball court in Copán. The side walls have a long slope, whereas other ball courts
may have more nearly vertical walls.

Ball-court marker from Chichén Itzá, showing two ball players wearing protective equipment.

To shield themselves from the impact of the heavy rubber ball, Maya players wore protective equipment consisting of a broad belt of leather or wickerwork, and hip and knee pads. In the Highland area and in Veracruz, similar equipment was made of stone, presumably a ceremonial version of the practical equipment. A few of these stone objects have been found in the Lowlands—for example, at Palenque. The sixteenth-century manuscript of the *Popol Vuh* describes mythical twins playing ball with the lords of the Underworld. Since the twins represented astronomical bodies and the lords the forces of night, this symbolism of light conquering darkness must have been the primary significance of the game.

There are fifteenth- and sixteenth-century Spanish accounts of a ball game; a similar game is played today in northern Mexico, although with-

out a formal court; ball courts and ball-game equipment have been excavated; and sculpture and pottery depict ball players and scenes from
mythical games. Thus, historical, anthropological, and archaeological
sources are pooled to reconstruct the past.

There are various other kinds of Maya construction. The sweat house
was a feature of Maya ceremonial centers. It was probably used in connection with the ball games and had ritual as well as therapeutic purposes. Reservoirs and stone-lined drains were also constructed, and there
were *chultunes,* chambers carved out of living limestone. In the Puuc
area of Yucatán, where there are no cenotes, the *chultunes* served as
water reservoirs; in the Petén, they seem to have been used for storage,
burial, and the disposal of trash. Possibly they were also used for ceremonial chambers or for sweat baths. Perhaps their original purpose was
the mining of the soft marl beneath the surface crust of limestone. There
is a vaulted aqueduct at Palenque that channels a stream underground
through the site. In areas where there were streams and rivers, bridges
were sometimes built, and tunnels and breakwaters were constructed to
divert floods.

Sometimes gates were erected at ceremonial centers, and in spite of
the lack of wheeled traffic and draft animals there were roads, or causeways, the beds of which were made of large boulders and concrete, with
a surface of stucco or plaster. Sometimes the roads were flanked by low
walls or parapets. The longest road, on the Yucatán peninsula, was sixty-
two miles long and thirty feet wide. Sometimes the roads led from one
site to another; others simply connected precincts within the site. They
were surely built chiefly for ceremonial purposes and were, of course,
made for pedestrian traffic, although the litter was used to some extent by
the nobility.

Some sites have unusual edifices. In the area at the northern border
of the Central area there was a convention of building towers that looked
like pyramids with temples on the tops; but the steps of these pseudo-
pyramids are too steep to climb and the temples have blocked doorways
with no interior rooms. In other regions there were other kinds of towers.
The palace at Palenque boasts a four-story square tower with an interior
staircase and ceilings of wooden beams. One of the most impressive
examples of Maya architecture is the Hieroglyphic Staircase at Copán
which led up a stepped pyramid to a temple at the top. The risers of the
sixty-two steps, attaining a total height of about ninety feet, were solidly
decorated with about two thousand glyphs, the longest recorded Maya

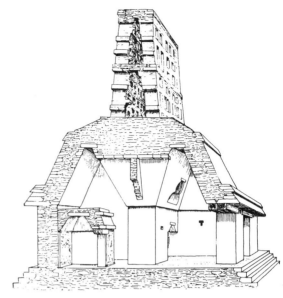

The Temple of the Cross at Palenque.

Group of temples at Palenque, showing roof-comb construction.

text known. At intervals in the center of the staircase stood five figures of gods or kings, about six feet high. On either side was a balustrade carved with a bird-and-serpent motif. In the Late Classic period this staircase must have been a truly glorious sight. Hieroglyphic staircases exist in a number of other Maya sites, but these are usually rather small and not decorated with sculpture. That at Copán is by far the largest and most splendid.

The dwellings around the centers and scattered throughout the countryside were, in contrast, simple. They usually had one or two rooms, were rectangular—although they often had rounded corners—and were placed on platforms that were sometimes faced with stone. The walls were made of stone rubble and plaster or of poles lashed with vines and sometimes plastered with clay or lime mortar. The roofs were of palm thatch, and the floors were frequently of plaster or gravel. This same kind of construction can be seen in the houses scattered throughout the countryside in Yucatán today. Modern Maya houses look very much like the sculptured representations of houses on the façades of the Classic Maya city of Uxmal. The house platforms, judging from their remains, seem to have been more soundly constructed in Classic times than they are today.

The palace at Palenque, showing the tower.

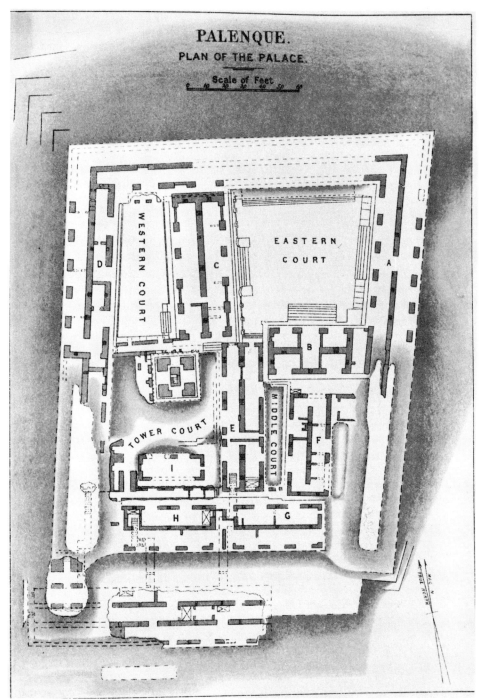

PALENQUE.

PLAN OF THE PALACE.

Scale of Feet

WESTERN COURT

EASTERN COURT

D

C

A

B

TOWER COURT

MIDDLE COURT

E

F

I

H

G

FROM A DRAWING BY A. P. MAUDSLAY

Plan of the palace at Palenque.

In the Classic period several houses were centered around a court, and there may have been more than one resident family. Some of the buildings may have been kitchens or other such service buildings. These clusters are fairly near each other and are close enough to a ceremonial center so that a farmer could walk there and back within a single day to deliver his produce, attend ceremonies, or even work on the monumental buildings.

The cities reflect many levels of Maya life. Cities were often near trade routes or rivers or agricultural plains; there were practical reasons for putting them where they are. There were also undoubtedly religious reasons—sacred springs or mountains or waterfalls, or other magic places.

The cities also reflect change. Although many concepts remained much the same over long periods of time, Maya cities are also witness to shifts in Maya thought and social structure. The Classic period saw the development of the power of god-kings, a power that undoubtedly began in the Early Classic period when palace-type buildings began to be

A modern Maya house, showing both rubble and pole construction.

PHOTOGRAPH COURTESY OF THE PEABODY MUSEUM, HARVARD UNIVERSI

Detail of building façade at Uxmal, showing a mask above a replica of a house.

erected. By the Late Classic period, it is clear that great buildings and monuments were constructed to honor Maya kings, who seem to have been identified with deities. By the Post-Classic, this kind of social structure died away and was replaced by a society that did not hold kings so dear or so sacred, did not erect stone monuments or massive buildings, but, instead, constructed small shrines, like token remnants of the previous architectural glories. These people probably traded widely, and produced a wealthy merchant class and a more egalitarian society. They were not motivated to put tremendous effort into splendid ceremonial centers. The great monuments of the past still stood, but those that were kept in use were marred by crude walls and blocked doorways, and those that were abandoned did not have long to wait before the forest began to take over the stones and mortar.

IV.
AGRICULTURE
AND TRADE

A modern farmer looking for land to cultivate could hardly imagine a less likely setting than the tropical rain forest in which the great Maya centers rose. Many people have thought that one of the greatest mysteries of the Maya culture is how it came to develop at all in a region where there is not only little natural wealth but a constant struggle against nature, with only stone tools and fire to fight the ever-encroaching forest. It was difficult enough to construct the great ceremonial centers, and there was an additional problem of how to support the population that built and then lived near them.

The Maya were, however, an agriculturally oriented people, highly observant of nature in general and plant life in particular, studying it and making the most of its resources. Whereas in the Old World, people domesticated many animals and relatively few plants, the situation in the New World was exactly reversed. The Classic Maya, like other ancient Americans, had very few domesticated animals—they had turkeys, dogs, ducks, and bees—but their list of plants is impressively rich, especially when compared to the list of plants domesticated in Europe at the same period.

Maize, or corn, was the basic staple crop of the New World. Botanists agree that high civilization in the New World developed in connection with the cultivation of maize. Wild maize was indigenous to the New

World. The oldest wild maize pollen yet known was found by archaeologists taking core drillings in the lake beds on which Mexico City is built, and is estimated to be about eighty thousand years old, predating human occupation in the New World by tens of thousands of years. Early nomadic peoples gathered wild maize and gradually domesticated and hybridized it. The oldest domesticated maize yet found in Mesoamerica comes from a valley southeast of Mexico City; by carbon-14 dating, it is thought to be about fifty-six hundred years old. Beans and squash were also cultivated by the people of Mesoamerica—maize, beans, and squash have been called the American Trinity—but maize is basic. Botanists have listed a hundred and fifty varieties of Indian maize, and even today it constitutes about three fourths of the Mesoamerican diet.

FROM A DRAWING BY A. P. MAUDSLAY

Detail from the main panel in the Temple of the Cross at Palenque, showing maize with a human head, emerging from a *Strombus* shell.

Maize is a dominant theme in Mesoamerican life, especially among the Maya. A period of abstinence was observed during the time it was planted, and offerings were made in the fields. The Maya did not go to war during the planting season, as maize came first. It was used for ceremonial or burial offerings, and it appears frequently as a symbolic and decorative motif in Classic Maya art. Its importance is indicated by the creation myth in the *Popol Vuh*, which states that the first man was made from maize:

> After that they began to talk about the creation and the making of our first mother and father; of yellow corn and of white corn they made their flesh; of corn-meal dough they made the arms and the legs of man. Only dough of corn meal went into the flesh of our first fathers, the four men, who were created.

Maize was regarded as the greatest gift of the gods and was itself venerated; there was a maize god, and the plant was also an attribute of the earth god. The descendants of the ancient Maya still address it as "Your Grace."

A great deal is known about how the ancient Lowland Maya raised maize. On the Yucatán peninsula, agricultural methods used today by the descendants of the ancient Maya must be very much like those of Classic times. The method is called slash-and-burn, or swidden agriculture, or *milpa* farming, derived from the Aztec word for cornfield. At the beginning of the dry season, in December or January, brush and trees are cleared with axes. In March or April the field is burned and the ashes of the fire are used to fertilize the ground. Then, in May or June, seeds are planted among the charred stumps of the trees. The Maya did not invent the plow; not only were there no draft animals to pull it but the shallow, rocky soil made it impractical. They used instead a digging stick for planting, not turning up the whole field but only making holes for the seeds. The digging stick is still the most efficient tool for this area. During the summer rainy season the fields are weeded once or twice, but they are given little other attention until the fall. When the grain is ripe, the stalks are bent to keep out the moisture, and the ears of maize are left to harden. Maize and other seed foods are stored in the fields in granaries called *chultunes*.

The difference between modern and Classic-period agriculture is that the axe used for clearing is now made of metal instead of stone, and the digging stick now has a metal point. The fields were formerly weeded

by hand, whereas now they are weeded with a machete. High tempera-
tures and heavy rainfall produce a rapid, luxuriant growth of weeds, and
weeding becomes more difficult the longer a field is used. The farmer
constantly faces the problem of competition from the growth of natural
vegetation as well as exhaustion of the soil.

A field cultivated by slash-and-burn methods can be used only for a
limited time before the soil begins to lose its fertility and the thick growth
of weeds and grasses becomes too competitive. In some Maya areas it is
feasible to use a field for only one year before abandoning it; in other
places it can be used for two or three years. Where the soil washes down
in light rainfall from the Puuc Hills, however, fields can be used from six
to twelve years. Maya farmers periodically have to find new land to clear
and plant, letting the old land lie fallow for a number of years—the time
needed for the woody growth to win out over the grasses—before they
can successfully plant the same land again. Research on present-day
methods in the Central area indicates that if a field is used for a single
crop it is usually allowed to rest for four years; if it is used for two
successive crops, it lies fallow for six to seven years. In some areas two
crops can be harvested on the same land in a single year. The type of soil
and vegetation and the pressure of the dependence on the land determine its use.

It has been estimated that the Central area could support a population of a hundred to two hundred people per square mile with this kind
of farming. Since the farmer had to work in the fields only when his crop
needed tending and could produce about twice the maize requirement of
the average family, adequate food could be produced and still leave a
considerable labor force of either nonfarmers or farmers who could have
worked in the ceremonial centers during the parts of the year when their
crops did not need tending. The crop yield in the drier Northern area is
somewhat less than that in the Central area.

It has been argued that this kind of agriculture destroys timber and
can cause deforestation and erosion, and that the burning destroys the
humus in the soil. Slash-and-burn agriculture, however, generally con-
serves soil fertility because the forest cover that returns during fallow
periods tends to produce a high organic content in the soil. Studies have
been made of present-day slash-and-burn agriculture in the region, and
the Carnegie Institution has also done experimental farming in Yucatán,
using ancient tools and methods. Other studies have been made of similar
agricultural methods still used in other parts of the world, in Africa and

Asia. The purpose of these studies is to determine the capabilities and limitations of this type of agriculture in supporting the Classic Maya population, for modern agricultural experts disagree on whether or not such a primitive form of agriculture could have supported the population of the large Lowland Maya centers.

One serious limitation of this method, of course, is that it requires a relatively large amount of land. It has been suggested that swidden agriculture can sustain only a shifting population, which, in the case of the Classic Maya, would have meant a tenuous support for the ceremonial centers and the large estimated population. There is now a general feeling among scholars that the Maya must have turned to other forms of agriculture, as well as swidden farming.

In a number of places in the Lowlands, remains of various kinds of terracing have long been known, and relic raised fields have recently been found. In raised fields, platforms of earth are lifted from low, damp, or seasonably inundated soil, so that the water runs in drainage canals around the fields. Higher, hillside country that is subject to erosion can be utilized if the soil is saved by terracing. Kitchen gardens have also been cited as likely ways of extending food production, and it has been suggested that the ramon tree was a major source of food in Classic times. The tree is productive and its fruit nutritious; moreover, it can be stored in *chultunes*. Other suggestions have been that some food was imported from the Highlands, or that the Maya also practiced other forms of agriculture, such as *chinampas*, the so-called floating gardens that existed in the Aztec area, some of which can be seen near Mexico City today. The lakes and swamps of the Petén might have supported such an agriculture, but as yet no archaeological evidence has been found for it, although a number of writers have noted that many Maya sites are located near swamps, or *bajos*, which may have been used in some agricultural technique.

The study of Maya agricultural life is based on existing methods, archaeological finds, botanical and geographical observations, and sixteenth-century sources, many of which are quite detailed, but tell of customs in a less populous time. Some of these customs can be projected back to the Classic period, but allowances must be made for a great deal of change. Although many observations and studies have been made, the overall picture is still unclear. Yet many details are known.

The maize was prepared by boiling or soaking it in lime water and then draining it in a gourd colander. While it was still wet, it was ground on a *metate*—a small stone table—with a *mano*, a cylindrical handstone. The resulting paste was most commonly mixed with water to make *pozole*, a thin gruel, or formed into cakes, the still familiar *tortillas*, which were roasted on a flat pottery griddle and eaten with beans or chili. On special occasions chocolate was mixed with ground maize and spiced with chili.

Beans and squash were often planted in the same hole with the maize or in the rows between. There were numerous varieties of squash and pumpkin, and two varieties of beans, a red one and a black one. A traveler in the area today is aware of the ubiquitous *frijole*. Chili peppers, tomatoes, yucca, and sweet potatoes were also sometimes planted in the same field. Many of the foods of the Maya, both ancient and modern, are strange to us, such as manioc, chaya, and jicama; but other fruits and vegetables are found in today's supermarkets—avocados, sweet potatoes, guavas, and tomatoes—or are the sources of such familiar foods and seasonings as vanilla beans, chili peppers, and, of course, chocolate, which is made from the cacao bean. Several important food plants may have been developed by the Maya—cacao, manioc, the papaya, and the avocado pear—while jicama may have been introduced into the Maya area in Post-Classic times.

Cacao beans were an important item. In Post-Classic times they were currency in Mesoamerica, as wampum was in parts of North America. Although the beans can be dried, stored, and easily carried and shipped, they can only be grown in certain areas. They need well-drained land, rainfall, and limited sunlight, and constant vigilance is necessary as they ripen to keep marauding animals away. In the Classic period they were grown on the Pacific slopes of the Highland area and at the western edge of the Central area in Tabasco and Chiapas, and they may also have been grown in British Honduras. For the most part, chocolate was a luxury, as most of the cacao crop probably went to the priests and nobles and the surplus was traded for the products of other areas.

Most of the secondary food crops of the Central area were fruits, which were produced during a short season and could not be stored. Many of the indigenous trees produce fruit, and they were also planted around houses. The breadnut tree, an important food source particularly in times of crop failure, is frequently found around the ruins. Other trees, both wild and domesticated, found in the area included hog plums, nance plums, and guavas. The papaya was domesticated, as the wild papaya is not edible.

Not all plants, of course, were grown for food. Some were used for dyes such as indigo, and others were used for utensils; for example, the calabash, a large gourd, was used for cups, bowls, and colanders. Cotton was grown in the drier areas in the North and was an important trade product for the Yucatecans, both as raw material and as woven cloth. Agave, used to make fiber, also came from Yucatán, and today it is the source of the modern sisal, or henequen, fiber. Maguey was grown for fiber in the Guatemalan Highlands.

The jungle itself provided many useful products. Wood was used for the poles of dwellings and the beams of temples. The sapodilla tree, the source of chicle for chewing gum, gave the Lowland Maya wood for the carvings that decorated their buildings. Mahogany was used as a building material. Palm trees were used in a number of ways. Their leaves were used for roof thatch, fire fans, baskets, and rain cloaks, and the fruit of certain palms was used for food. Rubber trees were also important. Concentrated in some areas and scattered through the jungle in others, they provided the Maya with rubber for their balls, rain-proofing for capes, and material to be traded with the non-rubber-producing Highlands. The copal tree, which grows wild in the Lowlands and was found in groves in Yucatán at the time of the Conquest, produces a resin that was burned for incense in Maya temples, and was also used to make small objects that have been found in burials and in the Sacred Cenote at Chichén Itzá. Cakes of copal, a dark-amber-colored semitransparent substance, were decorated with cross-hatching and painted blue. Sometimes copal was molded in the shape of a heart to be offered for sacrifice. Other trees, such as logwood and Brazil wood, were used to make dyes, while still another, the liquidambar, produces a resin which was used as a perfume as well as an adhesive. The inner bark of a wild fig tree was beaten to make paper.

Not only did plant life provide the Maya with food, clothing, shelter, and the materials of art, it also provided medicine. The Spaniards were greatly impressed by the Maya uses of herbs and roots with medicinal properties: "There is no disease to which the native Indians do not apply plants," the *Relaciones de Yucatán* states. Some of the plants mentioned in sixteenth-century manuscripts are recognized today as having pharmaceutical properties, but the curative value of many of them is dubious. Cures made from plants were either taken internally or applied externally, in various ways, and were accompanied by magic spells and incantations, for sickness was ascribed to supernatural causes. Chili, honey, and other ordinary foods were sometimes part of the compounds.

In contrast with the rich profusion of plant life used by the Maya, there was little domesticated livestock. The Classic Maya raised dogs and turkeys for food, and in Yucatán several varieties of ducks were raised for their feathers and exported to other areas. The Maya in Yucatán were also beekeepers. Wild honey was gathered in the woods, and most families kept hives of small stingless native bees. The hives, set on sloping racks under a thatched roof, were made of hollowed sections of tree trunk, the ends of which were closed with a piece of wood or stone sealed in place with mud so that it could be easily removed to get the honey. The bees entered through a small hole in the side. This method of agriculture, described by sixteenth-century writers, had probably been in existence for centuries; it still goes on in Yucatán today. Both the wax and the honey, which is thin, delicate, and delicious, were highly prized and were among the principal trade items of the Yucatec. The wax was used for various ceremonial purposes, although apparently not for candles. Fermented honey and water, in which the pounded bark of the balche tree was soaked and to which maize or tree roots were sometimes added, made a fermented beverage that was drunk by the ancient Maya on ceremonial occasions. There are sixteenth-century reports of other intoxicating beverages, all of them with a honey base. Travelers in Yucatán today will be offered xtabentun, a modern distilled liqueur made from honey, that has the flavor of a delicate anisette.

Although domesticated animals were scarce, there was considerable wild life. The Maya hunted in the grassy savannas that dot the Lowland jungle, using traps or spears; the bow and arrow were not introduced until after the Classic period. The Maya was a considerate hunter, killing only what he needed. Even today, when the modern Maya kills a deer, he apologizes to it. "I have need," he explains to the animal he has killed. In addition to deer, the ancient Maya hunted birds (shot with pellets from a blow gun), wild turkeys, curassows, wild boar, rabbits, peccaries, and armadillos. Other sources of protein were fish, turtles, iguanas, and insects. There were fresh-water fish, and Yucatán, with its long seacoast, provided salt-water fish that could be dried or salted for shipment. The Yucatán coast also produced shells for ornaments and for trading.

Landa described the diet of the sixteenth-century Maya as follows. In the morning they drank a hot gruel of finely ground maize, and during the day they drank liquids, either watered-down gruel or a foaming beverage made from ground maize and cacao or from ground maize spiced with chili pepper. In the evening they ate stews of vegetables and deer meat, fish, or the meat of wild or tame birds. For special feasts they had roasted fowl, bread, and a drink made from cacao.

Design from a polychrome vase depicting a ceremony involving a deer. The men carry spears, and one of them is blowing on a conch shell. The scene may relate to hunting.

Deer trapped in a snare.

Animals were killed not only for food. The jaguar skin was a sign of rank, and the pelts of jaguar and deer were cured and softened to be used by warriors and chiefs. Feathers were used to ornament clothing. The beautifully colored plumage must have added greatly to the glory of Maya dress and accessories, for the Maya used toucans, parrots, hummingbirds, herons, and occasional macaws. The long, colorful feathers of the quetzal bird, from Highland Guatemala, were the most spectacular and treasured.

Each of the Maya areas provided valuable resources, but the productive heart of the Maya country was the Central Lowland area. At first glance, the rain forest would seem to be a great impediment to the development of a civilization. Yet this Central area is neither as high and cold as the mountainous Southern area, nor as arid as the Yucatán peninsula; actually it is capable of producing more crops—and more varieties of crops—than either of the other areas. The peripheral areas tended to produce specialty crops, but the Central area had natural profusion and variety. The very richness of its teeming growth gave the people who inhabited it a vast supply of vegetal raw materials for their livelihood and trade. The simple fact that the important centers of the Classic period did exist in the jungle is the best argument for its ability to support the civilization. Also, of course, the geographical variety of the over-all Maya area was of tremendous advantage in affording the Maya such a variety of materials and foods. Although they lacked many things that modern man cannot imagine being without, their environment provided them with numerous useful objects that they traded not only among themselves but probably with other areas of Mesoamerica, enabling them to have a rich and complex culture.

Goods were certainly traded throughout Maya history. At the time of the Conquest certain goods served as a sort of currency, chiefly cacao beans and beads of a red shell that was found along the Pacific coast. These must have been trade items, if not currency, in the Classic period, and jade beads may also have been a kind of money. At the time of the Conquest small copper hatchets and bells were also used for exchange.

The history of trade in the New World is probably very long, and merchants occupied a special place in Mesoamerican life. In the Pre-Classic period the Olmec evidently traded over wide areas. In the Post-Classic period the *pochteca*, the Aztec merchants, were a highly organized and esteemed group, valuable to the Aztec state for their knowledge of other peoples, other areas, and the sources of supply for various

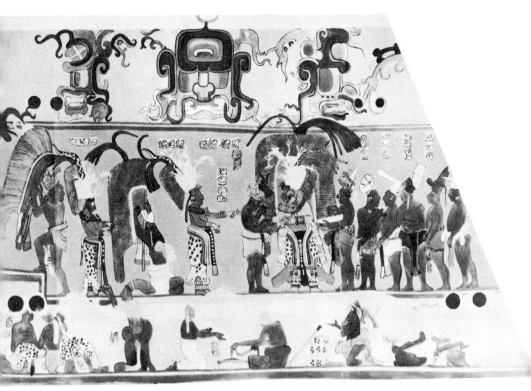

AFTER A PAINTING BY ANTONIO TEJEDA; REPRODUCED BY PERMISSION
OF THE CARNEGIE INSTITUTION OF WASHINGTON

Wall painting at Bonampak, depicting a ritual that utilized goods resulting from trade.

products. Merchants were powerful allies of the military chiefs and the nobles, and were an important element in the expansion of the Aztec empire. Aztec merchants went in advance of Aztec conquest. They were not merely merchants, which made them rich; they were spies whose valuable information made them powerful.

Much less is known of the activities of the Classic Maya merchant. Presumably the Maya were not so interested in territorial expansion as the Aztec were, and since the Maya merchant for the most part dealt not only with friendly areas but with people who spoke the same language, his role was probably different from that of his Aztec counterpart. Nevertheless, he may have served the same functions in some degree. There is evidence that Maya trade was well organized and a vital part of the life of the community, and merchants may well have been persons of social and economic substance. Sixteenth-century accounts state that Maya merchants of the time ranged from wealthy nobles—including the son of one of the last city rulers in the Northern area—to the itinerant peddler with his pack on his back.

There is much archaeological evidence of a rich trade among the Maya from early times. There are a great number of shells and stingray spines in early burials at Tikal, which is far inland, and shells from the Pacific coast have been found in Lowland sites. Quartzite, a material probably imported from British Honduras, has also been found in pre-Classic layers at Tikal. Flint implements were probably given in return, for Tikal is rich in flint. Obsidian also appears in some of the earliest burials in the Petén, although it is not indigenous to the area. Obsidian, a volcanic glass, is found in the Highland region and was traded as a raw material.

Metates and *manos* of lava and other volcanic stone have been found in the Petén and must have come from the Highlands. Cinnabar, the powdered red coloring found so frequently on Lowland jades, also comes from volcanic areas. Pottery was an item of trade, indicated by the fact that the pottery of one area has been found in the burials of another, and many of the pigments and tempers used in the making of pottery were probably also traded.

Jades carved in the distinct style of one area have been found in other places. Thus far, jade has been discovered *in situ* in only one location in the area, eastern Guatemala. The Maya probably most frequently found jade in the form of pebbles or boulders in stream beds, which is suggested by the water-worn appearance of the uncut surfaces of jade objects. Most jade must have come from the Highlands and was traded to the Lowlands, and there seems to have been further trading in which the finished carvings were traded back to the Highlands, because jades carved in Lowland style have been found in the Highland area.

There must have been a great deal of trading by sea, from Tabasco around the Yucatán peninsula to the Gulf of Honduras. There are sixteenth-century Spanish accounts of encountering large dugout canoes with sails making their way around the coast, laden with a variety of goods. They probably traveled considerable distances, trading items at each port. Heavier goods would surely have been transported by sea whenever possible, since the only land transportation was manpower. Stone objects such as the distinctive marble vases from Honduras must have been carried by sea, and some timber may have been transported in this way. In the sixteenth century salt from deposits along the northern coast of Yucatán was an important trade item, as it must have been in earlier times, and it was probably transported by water since it is heavy. The salt trade undoubtedly helped link Yucatán with the Gulf coast of Mexico. Bishop Landa writes that during sixteenth-century feuding among the people of Yucatán the coastal people would not give salt or fish to the inland people, and the inland people did not let the coastal people have game or fruit. This must have been a great hardship, for apparently people whose main diet is plants crave more salt than meat eaters. There were also inland waterways that carried trade in the sixteenth century, and these surely dated back to Classic times.

Although few ancient roads are known in the Maya area, it is quite possible that there were other causeways existing in the Classic period that have not yet been discovered. The roads that are known were not in use at the time of the Conquest, when there were only rough trails through the brush and jungle. Certainly these trails were well marked, however, as they were used by merchants carrying smaller, lighter freight. The wealthier merchants rode in litters. Trade items were carried by tumpline, a kind of net bag worn around the head and carried on the back. The feather trade was probably carried mostly overland, as were cakes of copal in cornhusk containers. Vanilla, maize, and chili were probably traded from the Lowlands to the Highlands, and possibly, at least in times of Lowland crop failure, maize may have been brought in from the Highlands.

At the time of the Conquest there was a Maya god to whom homage was paid by both merchants and travelers. Landa wrote that travelers "carried incense on their journeys and a little dish to burn it in, so that at night, wherever they came they erected three small stones, and placed on each several grains of incense, and in front they placed three other flat stones on which they threw incense." This god was also worshiped in rites performed by the owners of cacao plantations, an appropriate connection because cacao was a form of money. The plantation owners sacrificed a dog to this deity and made offerings of incense and iguana.

Markets must have played an important and colorful part in Mesoamerican life. There was a great Post-Classic market at Chichén Itzá, and it is known that there were other important markets in this period in Yucatán. A sixteenth-century Guatemalan source stated that the rulers took great care that there should be very rich fairs and markets, which were held close to the temples. Maize was exchanged for beans, beans for cacao, and salt for spices.

Some ceremonial centers are rich in trade items; others seem to have

Late Classic polychrome vase from Highland Guatemala, showing a man being carried in a litter.

Carved marble vase from the Ulua Valley, Honduras. Ten inches high. Such objects were trade items.

had relatively little trade. This variation relates to their importance, their proximity to trade routes, and the self-sufficiency of their own economy. But certainly trade was an important part of Maya civilization. It not only made possible a fairly high standard of living but reinforced the cultural and political ties between people of the various parts of the area.

A good deal of recent archaeological work has concentrated on the east coast of the Yucatán peninsula, that is, from Quintana Roo, in Mexico, down through Belize to Honduras. One of the main focuses of this work has been on sea trade along this coast, which probably had its origin in Veracruz or Tabasco. It is now felt that, during the Classic period, there was an emphasis on overland trade, whereas in the Post-Classic period coastal trade was particularly flourishing. It has also been posited that Classic trade was more a matter of prestige goods for the ruling classes, whereas the Post-Classic trade dealt more in staples for a more secular, or more democratic, society. But there was surely a mixture of goods in both eras. In the relatively modest Post-Classic coastal sites, exotic materials—pyrite, jade, obsidian, and pottery from northwest Yucatán—were found.

The land-then-sea pattern correlates, in general, with building patterns. Classic centers are, for the most part, inland, whereas there was a building boom on the East Coast in the Post-Classic period. This is not to say that the East Coast was completely unimportant or uninhabited in early times, for Pre-Classic material has been recently found in several of the essentially Post-Classic sites, and there is also one very large and important Classic site, Cobá, near the east coast of Quintana Roo, where mapping, clearing, and consolidation have recently been in progress.

As there was increasing sea trade, there was also increasing piracy and raids made from the sea—or such is the argument used to explain an inland population shift in certain coastal sites. Nevertheless, it appears that, when the Spaniards arrived on the scene, they interrupted a thriving coastal commerce.

V.
ARTISANS
AND ARTIFACTS

Raw materials and artifacts traveled along Maya trade routes, and so did ideas and art styles. In the Early Classic period, for example, a certain type of monumental sculpture was diffused along the trade-route waterways of the Central area, a fact attested to by the style of the sculptures themselves and the dates on them. Sculpture was an important product of the Classic period, and it is now an important source of information to the archaeologist.

The most interesting sculptures are the stelae that were carved throughout the Central area during the Classic period. These are rectangular stone panels, usually from about 5 to 12 feet tall, although some are over 30 feet high. They were placed in front of important buildings in the main plazas of ceremonial centers. Each one bears the date of its dedication as part of its hieroglyphic text.

A single masculine figure in ceremonial regalia dominates the design on most stelae. The figure—elaborately dressed and equipped, and usually standing—is, in most instances, known to be a ruler. The dress of the figure varies, and therefore the stelae are an excellent source of knowledge about actual clothing and ornaments that no longer exist. Variations in the type and depiction of costume can also help in tracing the progressive styles of the stelae, for such details change slowly and subtly through the Classic period, both in the manner of depiction and in the dress itself.

The basic garment is a loincloth that usually terminates in an apron in the front, but some of the figures wear short skirts or kilts, the original of which was made of cloth or jaguar skin, and still others wear long skirts. Capes are represented that may have been made of tubular beads or feathers as well as cloth and there are sometimes mantles that reach from the shoulder to the ground. Also depicted are shirts of cloth or

Late Classic altar and stela at Tikal. The figure is wearing an elaborate headdress and a jaguar kilt, and holds a ceremonial bar.

PHOTOGRAPH COURTESY OF THE UNIVERSITY MUSEUM, PHILADELPHIA

jaguar skins. The most striking part of the costume is usually the elaborate headdress, made of feathers and jade and other ornaments, and sometimes decorated with a mask. An object so ornate and top-heavy may not actually have been worn, but only symbolically represented on the sculpture. Stela figures also wore ear ornaments, necklaces or collars, belts, wrist and ankle ornaments, and sandals.

Early Classic sculpture seems to have been preoccupied with the symbolic character of the subject matter. The forms are simply and statically represented. There is a generally similar style in this period, which appears to have been diffused out from the Petén, where the earliest stelae have been found at Tikal and Uaxactún.

On Early Classic stelae a single masculine figure stands on the front and a hieroglyphic inscription is carved on the back or sides. Usually the figure is depicted with his shoulders in front view and his head and the lower part of his body in profile. The feet are placed one behind the other, with the weight evenly placed.

In the latter part of the sixth century there was a strange hiatus in the making of sculpture. Few monuments have been found from this period, and the absence of stelae is particularly noticeable. Those that are known come from peripheral sites, not from the heart of the Central area. It appears that many early stelae were mutilated or destroyed at this time. Then, at the end of the sixth century, the activity of stela making began again, and there was a difference in style and approach. The Petén no longer dominated, and each area now had its own distinctive style. This change in sculpture coincided with changes in the techniques of masonry construction and styles of pottery. It seems likely that some historical event was responsible for both the temporary cessation of stela carving and the subsequent change in art forms generally, but what this event might have been is another of the Maya mysteries. In any case, this change marks the difference between the Early and Late Classic periods.

After A.D. 600 there was a larger number of stelae than ever before, indicating a period of prosperity and peaceful activity. At the beginning of the Late Classic period the emphasis shifted from the subject matter— that is, the subject matter as religious symbolism—to the quality of the details, the clothing, the ornaments, and the decorative scrolls. Maya art is a combination of realistic human and animal forms with highly stylized, sometimes grotesque, symbolic forms. The style in the Late Classic period became more elaborate and eventually, toward the end of the Classic period, it was concerned with the over-all composition. Toward

PHOTOGRAPH BY A. P. MAUDSLAY

the end of the seventh century there was again a similarity of art styles throughout the area, although sites retained certain local characteristics.

Generally the figures in Late Classic stelae are either standing with both feet pointing outward or in full profile with one leg obscured by the other. There is never a great deal of motion in Maya sculpture, but these poses suggest more movement than the earlier static stelae designs. Whereas in Early Classic designs the busyness of the details of the design gives whatever sense of motion exists, in later sculpture movement is suggested in the action or pose of the figures; for example, many of these figures lean slightly or bend at the waist.

The major figures often hold symbolic objects. Sometimes it is a ceremonial bar, which often has, on either end, the head of a deity who is associated with accession to power, or it may have a snake head enclosing the head of another deity at either end. A variation is the manikin scepter, a dwarfish figure, who is frequently the accession god and has a foot ending in a serpent head. The main stela figure sometimes holds an elaborate bag. Sometimes he holds a shield, which may be decorated with a face mask and trimmed with feathers or tassels, and he may hold a spear, a staff, or a hafted knife.

Sometimes there are subsidiary figures who usually have somewhat different poses and types of dress and may hold different objects. These may often be ancestors, through whom power was inherited; they may sometimes be prisoners; or they may be the ruler shown in an earlier moment of a rite of purification. These figures are usually shown as smaller than the major figure, who is, at that time, more powerful than anyone else.

In a number of instances, the principal figure on a stela has been identified as a woman. These may have been women from a more important site who became wives of local rulers, or the mothers through whom kings inherited power; it is also possible that some of these women held power themselves. In other instances, female figures are shown paired with male figures. Women can be fairly easily identified by dress—they wear long skirts, long robes or tunics, or beaded skirts with short capes; they may also wear tubular ear ornaments and jade necklaces or collars. Much of this apparel can also be worn by men, so, in cases of doubt, it is useful that the glyph for "woman" is now known.

Stela inscriptions usually begin with the date of the dedication of the monument. Numerous dates within the text may note the birth, accession,

Stela at Quiriguá, over nineteen feet high, showing a king who, because of the elements in his name glyph, is nicknamed "Two-legged Sky."

Stela at Copán. The figure is carved almost in full-round, and there is a panel of glyphs at the side.

and death of the ruler. Sometimes dates appear to refer to occasions in the king's life, of whose meaning we are not sure. Sometimes ancestor lists are given in a seeming claim to legitimacy in power. The text was often placed on the back of the stela as well as on the front, and sometimes the design and text are wrapped around the sides.

The figures are carved in either high or low relief, although a few sites have sculpture that is almost in full round. A distinctive type at Piedras Negras, in which a figure sits in a niche, combines high and low relief. At Quiriguá, toward the end of the Classic period, huge zoomorphic boulders were carved like complicated monsters with human figures in their jaws, and long hieroglyphic inscriptions.

The year A.D. 731 saw the raising of more Maya monuments than any other time; this was a high point of Maya creativity. But in the next century there was a sharp falling off in the production of stelae. There was either a sudden cessation of stelae-making or a deterioration in the style and craftsmanship of the last ones made. Where stelae were produced, the intricate calendrical glyphs were abandoned and there is clear evidence of infiltration by outside influences. At Seibal and Altar de Sacrificios, on the southern edge of the Central area, non-Maya faces and non-Maya motifs appear on the last stelae. It was not only stela-making that was abandoned at this time, but also the making of other sculpture, artifacts, and architecture—it was the end of the great Maya period.

The Maya, of course, made many kinds of sculpture other than the stelae. Each stela was accompanied by a round stone "altar" that might have a greater range of possible designs than the stelae and usually did not include calendrical texts. Maya buildings themselves were richly decorated, and some of the finest existing examples of Maya sculpture are the lintels and wall panels that were part of the buildings. Heads tenoned into buildings, sculpture on roof combs, ball-court markers, and many other types of stone carving enriched Maya architecture. In Yucatán, Puuc architecture, named after the low-lying hills of the region, has façades elaborately decorated with colonnettes and various abstract designs. Sometimes a whole façade was covered with identical stone masks (usually of the rain god) placed close together over the entire surface to make a rich and intricate pattern. Maya art is florid and flamboyant and rarely allows simple statements or empty spaces.

This complex sculpture was made with the same kind of simple stone tools the architect used. The carving must have required a patience incomprehensible to modern craftsmen. Stone was, of course, not the

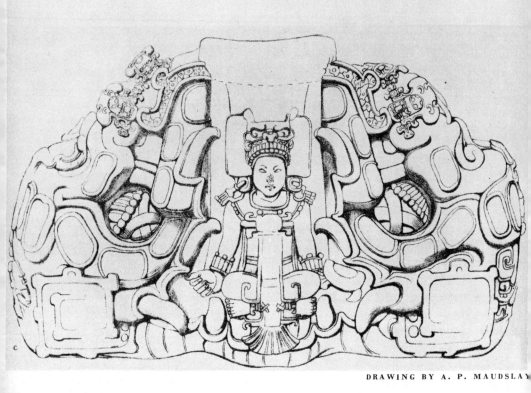

Giant zoomorph from Quiriguá, over seven feet high, showing a human figure seated in the coils of a monster deity.

only material used for sculpture; stucco made from lime was also used, and there was apparently considerable use of wood, although most of the wooden sculpture has deteriorated and disappeared.

The Maya were also highly skilled workers with jade, flint, shell, and bone. Although the cloth garments and feather ornaments depicted in Maya sculpture and painting have disappeared, various objects made of hard materials have endured. Jade was an especially important material: there were necklaces of jade beads, complicated ear ornaments made in several pieces, small jade ornaments to be attached or sewn to garments, nose ornaments, finger rings, bracelets, and, especially notable, pendants carved with representations of human figures. As in sculpture, the principal-figure motif dominates the design, although on the pendants the figure is often seated rather than standing. Jade objects were frequently covered with the fine red powder of cinnabar. The Maya made figurines, masks, and ornaments of jade mosaic often used with shell.

Detail of a carved wooden lintel from Tikal.

Jade was worked with remarkable skill. The stone tools used to work it probably included hammerstones, grinding stones, rasps, and solid drills. Thin saws of wood and hollow drills of reed or birdbone were probably also employed. Most of these tools were used with abrasives. Incising was done with jade, quartz, or flint tools. The objects were polished with jade tools or with wood and an abrasive—quartz sand or crushed jade. Openwork was begun with a drill and finished by string-sawing. Tools of jade may have been made not for ceremonial use, but simply because they were hard enough to work jade to make nonutilitarian objects.

The Aztec word for jade was the same as the word for "precious," and when gifts were given to the Spaniards in the sixteenth century it was jade, not gold, that the Indians considered the most valuable offerings. A jade bead was sometimes placed in the mouth of the deceased in Mesoamerican burials, for it assured that the dead man would obtain sustenance in the afterlife. This custom was followed in many Maya burials as well as those of other areas. Jade beads may also have been a form of money for the living. Worked jades are often found in Maya burials and caches, and the presence of unworked jade pebbles in hidden offerings suggests that the material itself had religious significance even before it was carved into any kind of object or effigy. The Maya used the same hieroglyphs for jade and that most precious element, water.

Pendants with seated figures were often carved from shell, and sometimes bone was incised with delicate carvings. Bracelets were constructed of small pieces of shell and bone. Mirrors were made from iron pyrites and were probably worn as ornaments, and there are also beads of iron pyrites. In addition to articles of apparel, numerous ceremonial objects have been found. Flint was chipped into elaborate abstract human and animal shapes. Obsidian was worked thin and then incised with designs or covered with painted stucco. Bowls with fluted sides were carved from onyx marble and were sometimes incised with figures and glyphs or covered with painted stucco. Maya artists were capable of creating the most delicate and finely crafted small objects as well as

Maya craftsmen included not only sculptors and lapidaries but painters. Building exteriors were painted and interiors were decorated with frescoed murals. Paint, of course, is fragile, and there is very little of it left, only enough to tell that there was once color on the façade of a building or a sculpture, only traces of shapes in paint on an inside wall. This is unfortunate, for, whereas Maya sculpture had a narrow range of

Late Classic carved shell pendant, four inches high. The drilled holes once contained jade inlays.

subject matter, mural painting was apparently much freer and more telling. Remains of paintings have been found in a number of Maya sites.

One of the most important discoveries in the Maya area was at the site of Bonampak in Mexico, near the Guatemalan border. Although the site had obviously been visited by the Lacandon Indians—who burned copal in the temples there, leaving their braziers as evidence—it was apparently unknown to any outsider until it was discovered and reported by chicleros in 1946. The first archaeologists to arrive made drawings of all the standing buildings except one, which they did not see because of the dense vegetation even though it is in the heart of the site. Later that same year this building was discovered, and when it was entered, its three rooms were found to be covered, walls and ceilings, with painted murals. The site was named Bonampak, a made-up Maya word meaning "painted walls."

In the murals, friezes of human figures are placed against solid-colored backgrounds that perhaps represent the setting of the scene

Wall painting from Bonampak, showing captives being brought before a chief.

depicted—the blue backgrounds, for instance, suggest the sky or the out-of-doors. The figures vary greatly in dress and pose, and some of the poses are rendered with remarkable naturalism, more so than in the formalized sculpture.

Some of the same characters appear in more than one scene in the three rooms. It has been suggested that the scenes may represent, first, preparations by dancers impersonating the gods of the earth, then a raid on a small settlement and the capturing and bringing back of prisoners, and finally a sacrificial ceremony and dance. Above the scenes are a series of masks and symbolic motifs. Paintings of scenes like these show objects used by the Maya—clothing, weapons, musical instruments, costumes of the dance, headdresses and ornaments of the nobles, etc. They depict methods of fighting and sacrifice. Because they show activities not normally recorded in sculpture, they give a glimpse into Maya ceremonial life. It is sad that there are so few mural paintings still extant. The

Bonampak murals were painted toward the end of the Classic period at a time when outside influences were felt in the Maya area, and the warlike activities represented in the paintings may represent, to some extent, ideals and methods imported from Mexico. The murals were damaged and covered with lime deposits when they were found; unfortunately, they have continued to deteriorate. However, careful copies of them have been made.

Maya painters also decorated pottery. Polychrome pottery is one of the distinguishing characteristics of the advent of the Classic period in the Central area. With it came the use of a more lustrous slip. Soft, low-fired wares were common to both the Highlands and Lowlands in the Classic period. Classic Maya pottery advances, especially in the Central area, were in decorative techniques rather than in improved serviceability. The pottery became more beautiful rather than more useful, but even the most elaborate polychrome tended to be technically inferior.

There were many methods of decoration. The bowls and vases of the Central area were of relatively simple shapes, but their walls were elaborately decorated. Polychrome pots were colored orange, red, black, brown, buff, gray, and cream. The pigments generally used for fired polychrome pottery were made from manganese and iron-manganese ores, clays, ferruginous clays, and hematite. Post-fired painting, applied over a stucco or plaster coating, utilized pigments like cinnabar, malachite, and azurite, which would be destroyed if they were fired. Because of their delicacy these vases were suitable for ritual use and for mortuary offerings for people of high rank in the religious hierarchy, but not for everyday use. Sometimes vases were not painted, but had figures carved into the walls of the pot; perhaps cinnabar red was later applied to the carving. "Maya blue" was used ritually for coloring temple frescoes, incense burners, and ceremonial vessels.

Early Classic pottery in the Maya Lowlands tended to have geometrical, stylized designs, often based on conventionalized creatures— such as toads, birds, and serpents—or on complicated scrolls. Like Early Classic sculpture, this pottery was fairly uniform in design throughout the Central area. This is true of the pottery found in house mounds as well as that from ceremonial centers. Again, the style, like the sculpture style, apparently was diffused from the Petén to other areas.

The Late Classic period produced a variety of pottery types and styles of decoration. The human figure was depicted quite naturalistically, but in certain conventional poses. Often there was a single seated

PHOTOGRAPH COURTESY OF
THE DUMBARTON OAKS COLLECTIONS

Bottom view of a carved pottery bowl that has double walls with rattles between them. Cinnabar has been rubbed in the carved design.

figure, similar to those represented on sculpture or jade pendants; this was particularly true of pots with carved decoration. Painted pots were often decorated with scenes in which some complicated symbolic ceremony was taking place. Supernatural creatures are depicted in some scenes. The major human figures in other scenes may be the same people who are depicted on sculpture.

The Highland Maya area is typified by effigy pots, usually in human shapes, as well as effigy incense burners. Polychrome techniques were not developed nearly as fully in the Highland area as they were in the Central area where brilliant decorative effects were achieved. Toward the end of the Classic period harder, more functional pottery began to be manufactured in the Highlands, and some of this was traded to the Lowlands.

No evidence of kilns has been found in Maya excavations, but surely the Classic Maya developed some means—perhaps a protective vessel—for keeping their polychrome from contact with the fuel in the process of firing. The potter's wheel was not known anywhere in the New World, and even today it is not generally used in Yucatán. Clay is modeled from a coil or slab, or a mass of wet clay is placed on a square block of wood that is turned by the feet of the potter, who sits modeling the jar with her hands—for pottery is mostly woman's work, as it probably was in Classic times. It is quite likely, however, that while women made the everyday ware, anything as important as fine ceremonial ware would have been made and decorated by male craft specialists.

In Late Classic times a variety of different pottery figurines appeared throughout much of the Lowland area. They often represent human beings in ceremonial regalia. Some of them are ball players wearing their protective equipment, others are warriors, dancing figures, or musicians. Sometimes they represent people dressed in ordinary clothing going about everyday activities, including women, often shown grinding corn on a metate. Some figures are seated on a throne or in a litter. There are other types of figurines that appear frequently: a woman with a child, an old man with a young woman, a hunchback, or a nude fat man. The faces and details of dress of figurines are usually quite naturalistic, often showing facial tattooing or scarification and bead ornaments stuck on the skin, as well as deformation of the head. Sometimes there are grotesque figures with anthropomorphic bodies and animal heads, representing either supernatural beings or men wearing animal masks. There are also various figurines representing animals: owls and other birds, jaguars, monkeys, and dogs. Although they are realistically depicted, they are frequently wearing necklaces or ear ornaments.

Although there is some overlap in the depiction of deities and enthroned figures, the cast of characters in the corpus of figurines is somewhat different from those shown in the codices, sculpture, or pottery. In spite of the everyday activities of many of them, these figures must have been considered objects of supernatural power. It seems inconsistent with Maya thought and motivation that they would have made such objects purely for decoration or to depict everyday ideas.

Many of these figurines are sound-producing. Some are whistles with a hole, or holes, to blow in or over, and others are rattles with a pellet of clay inside. It is possible that they were used to accompany ceremonial dances or processions; they may have been connected with sympathetic magic; or they may have been made without thought of using the sound

for a "practical" purpose, but with the idea that because air went through them and made sound, the figurines had a kind of life or animation.

The figurines were manufactured in various ways. Some are solid, some hollow. Some were entirely modeled by hand, while others were entirely mold-made, and often the front was made in a mold and the plain back was modeled by hand. Many of the figurines have free limbs that were attached to a mold-made torso, or the head was sometimes made in a mold and tenoned by a modeled neck to the body. Elaborate costume details were appliquéd. They were fired, and then most of them were painted. The best-known figurines—and generally the finest—come from the island of Jaina off the coast of Campeche. Jaina was a ceremonial center, but it is best known as a burial ground; it contained perhaps twenty-five thousand burials and has yielded a great deal of grave material, notably figurines. Jaina figurines are as handsome and delicate as any found in the ancient Old World and have, in fact, been compared in quality to the Tanagra figurines of Greece.

The painters who were most adept at decorating pottery vases may have been the same artists who painted the Maya codices, the folding-screen books of pounded bark covered with a thin sizing of lime and painted with pictures of deities and hieroglyphic texts.

Francisco Hernández, a sixteenth-century physician and naturalist in Mexico, describing the process of making paper, noted that "it is something like our paper, except that their paper is whiter and thicker, while ours is cheaper and heavier." Various species of wild fig trees were used. The larger branches were cut from the trees and left to soak all night on riverbanks so that they would soften. The following day the outer bark was removed and the inner bark was beaten with stone or wooden beaters until it was pliable, when it was cut into strips. The long strip was then folded like a screen and a coating of white lime was applied to both sides. Astronomical tables, portrayals of gods and ceremonies, and other religious lore were inscribed on it in hieroglyphs and pictures, in black and colors. The covers were made of decorative boards. These books must have been copied innumerable times through the centuries, for they contained the most important intellectual heritage of the Maya.

Three Maya codices have been known for a long time. They are all from the Post-Classic period, but at least one of them must be a copy of a Classic-period manuscript. A fourth codex has recently been found; its authenticity is still being debated by scholars.

Pottery figure of a seated woman in Jaina style. Sixteen and a half inches high.

Textile-weaving was apparently universal, but, since there are few remains, we can only guess at the exact nature of Maya cloth from representations in sculpture, painting, and figurines and from occasional shreds of cloth found in excavations. The cloth was woven of cotton or the fibers of the agave plant, and there were numerous sources of vegetable, animal, and mineral dyes. One assumes that women did the weaving, as they do in remote parts of the area today, using a loom with one end strapped to the waist and the other end attached to a tree or house post.

Metal, as has been mentioned, was unknown in the Classic period, or at least not until the end of the period, and the metal objects that have been found in the Maya area from the Late Classic and Post-Classic periods come from other areas. Metal was used chiefly for ornaments, although a few copper utensils have been found.

Maya artifacts have been found chiefly in excavations in the ceremonial centers, partly because there is more material there than in the house-mound groups, but also because more archaeological work has been done in the centers. The material comes chiefly from caches or offerings, from burials, and occasionally from trash mounds.

One of the most important things most archaeologists can find is a trash mound. Imagine an archaeologist of the future finding the well-preserved remains of a modern town dump or even the contents of a trash can; from these he could tell a great deal about what we eat and drink, the way food is packaged, the kinds of glasses and china we use, and many other useful bits of information from which he might begin to construct a picture of our civilization. The special importance of the trash mound, however, is that it gives information about the chronological sequence in the habitation of a site. For example, if one were to find a layer of trash from the 1920's below a layer of 1960 trash, one would have material that was not only descriptive but comparative.

Unfortunately, middens—or trash mounds—are rare in Maya sites. Because so much of the Lowland Maya area is limestone with a thin soil covering, it was necessary for the ancient Maya to salvage refuse dumps and use the material as fill under their plazas, in their mounds, or between floors. Thus the important task of relating objects according to the layer on which they are found in trash is quite difficult in the Maya area.

The Maya archaeologist's richest and most important finds come from caches and burials. Caches were groups of object offerings intentionally hidden under monuments or pavements or in structures. Caches have been found in Maya temples, palaces, platforms, and plazas as well as under stelae. When a stela was erected, a collection of objects was placed under or near it as a dedicatory offering. Caches vary from site to site. In the heart of the Central area Early Classic caches associated with stelae contain eccentric flints (in the forms of tridents, laurel-leaf blades, discs, etc.), eccentric obsidians, numerous obsidian fragments and flakes, flint flakes, and shells. Sometimes there were shell beads or small figurines of shell, pottery vessels, human teeth, and pieces of human bones. In a transitional period an improvement in craftsmanship is evident and there is greater variety in the shapes of eccentric flints and obsidians, and some of the obsidians were incised with designs. There were also pieces of unworked jade or jade beads. In the Late Classic period the contents of the caches under stelae tended to be rigidly prescribed. There were often nine eccentric flints, nine incised obsidians, and one to four pottery vessels, but rarely any jade. Caches under or in buildings were often quite different from those under stelae. Other cache material consists of iron pyrites, iron oxide (hematite), animal bones, and sting-ray spines. The caches found in buildings are also assumed to be dedicatory offerings.

The line between caches and burials is not always clear, for sometimes caches contain human remains while, on the other hand, some burials are incomplete because parts of the body were saved by survivors as relics. Burials also contain precious objects of jade, shell, bone, and pottery as grave offerings. To most archaeologists throughout the world, one of the most important finds is a grave. The care with which people were buried, the way they were buried, and the grave goods placed with them have been one of the best sources of artifacts and information. This is no less true in the New World, where it is obvious that people believed in a life after death and put equipment for this afterlife into the graves of the deceased.

In the Maya area graves are found in a great variety of places, and the dead were disposed of in a variety of ways. Bodies were inhumed or cremated. Burials in ceremonial buildings are common; they have been found in temples, palaces, under stairways, in walled-off rooms, in the pyramids themselves, and under plazas and altars as well as under house mounds, in *chultunes*, or simply in the ground. Graves were often cut out of bedrock or set within masonry construction; they were not filled with earth. The walls of tombs were sometimes painted or covered with stucco sculpture. Burial locations were significant—the more important the deceased, the more important the building in which he was buried—and the materials within were often of great value. In a rich burial the person may have been accompanied by other people, presumably sacrificial victims, as well as animals (alligator and turtle remains have been found). There were plain vessels containing foodstuffs, and there were elaborate vessels. Burial and cache pottery was usually either specially made or imported from another area. Sometimes a bowl was placed over the head of the deceased, and infants were often buried in pottery jars. In addition to the kinds of artifacts found in caches, burials have produced jaguar bones, bones of rodents and birds, pig and jaguar teeth, jaguar skins, strings of shells, onyx marble, copal, and, in at least one case, the remains of a codex. The body itself, if it was an important person, was richly decked with ornaments.

The recent excavations at Tikal have shown that sometimes when a building was being dismantled to make way for a new building or an addition to the old one, tombs with rich burials were discovered. The Maya apparently believed in the continuing power of the tomb, for they smashed and burned the grave offerings and then transported the burial material and reburied it.

One of the most impressive Maya burials was found in 1952 in the Temple of the Inscriptions at Palenque. A concealed staircase led down into the interior of the pyramid. Before arriving at the tomb itself archaeologists found several masonry boxes containing rich offerings— jade earplugs and beads, pottery, shells full of cinnabar, and a tear- shaped pearl. Outside the door of the tomb lay the skeletons of six young people. The tomb chamber itself was a large vaulted room containing nine great figures in stucco relief, slightly larger than life-size, that formed a procession around the walls. In the center lay a sarcophagus with a huge, elaborately carved stone lid. The skeleton inside was richly decked with jade jewelry, including a headdress, a necklace of jade beads in many forms, and elaborate, delicately incised jade earplugs. Over the breast lay a pectoral, around the wrists were bracelets of hundreds of jade beads, and on each finger was a great jade ring. At the time of burial the king—his name may have been Pacal—had been wearing a mask of jade mosaic with inlaid eyes of shell and obsidian, although the mask had slipped aside before it was found. In his hands he held great jade beads, in his mouth there was a jade bead, and at his feet lay other jade objects. Red cinnabar had been sprinkled over the body, the jade ornaments, and the interior sides of the sarcophagus, for the color red was associated with the east and the rising sun and may have been symbolic of rebirth.

Such a burial, aside from being an archaeologist's dream of discovery, tells a great deal about the mortuary customs of the Maya, and the excellence of Maya craftsmanship. Artists were probably highly trained craftsmen attached to the ceremonial centers, enjoying a special position in the Maya world. Certainly they had special technical skills and a sense of the importance of the art style and philosophy, and the sculptors must have been literate. Nevertheless, the Maya artist, although recognized for his skill and accorded a special place in the community, was still not important in himself, but only as the implement through which the gods and chieftains were honored.

Bishop Landa tells us that in the sixteenth century the creators of the images of the gods were confined to huts and not allowed visitors while they were working. They had to undergo a special ritual that consisted of burning copal, extracting their own blood as an offering, fasting, and maintaining continence. As the work progressed, the images of the gods were sprinkled with blood and incensed with copal. Landa's description, of course, postdates the Classic period by centuries, but the sixteenth-century ritual may bear some relationship to that of the earlier time.

Perhaps because of the nature of the social structure in which he lived, the Maya artist was conservative and changed his style and techniques only very slowly. The differences between Early and Late Classic stelae are hard to detect by one who has not examined hundreds of stelae, and, although style changes can be traced, there are no basic advances in the techniques by which these sculptures were made. Most of the technical advances of Maya craftsmen were in the direction of finer decoration rather than of functional improvements. This has been noted in the case of the potter and is also true to a large extent in the case of the architect. Although he developed superficial ways to increase the beauty and impressiveness of his buildings, over a period of hundreds of years he failed to make the simple step from the corbel vault to the true arch.

VI.
SCIENCE

The chief accomplishments of Maya science were in astronomy and mathematics. Their technical advances were small compared with their more abstract accomplishments. It is not easy for modern man to understand Maya science, for the Maya was not interested in astronomy and mathematics for the sake of pure science nor simply in relation to his everyday life or the recording of history; its purpose was largely for divination and the regulation of religious ritual. When the Maya recorded history they also foretold the future in terms of the past, and in putting together astronomical calculations and ritual cycles, they developed the most complex calendar in Mesoamerica.

An important part of this religious-scientific complex was the Maya's written language, the vehicle for working out problems and recording them. They were the only people in pre-Spanish America to have a developed form of writing, which they inscribed in books and on sculpture, vases, and other objects. People before them—the Olmec and the Zapotec people at Monte Albán—had a rudimentary form of writing, and later people—the Mixtec and Aztec—used only a handful of symbols. Most of the Maya books have been lost, but the Central area has an impressive quantity of date-bearing monuments. The largest number of sculptured texts found at any one site was at Copán, where there are over a hundred, counting the Hieroglyphic Stairway as a single text.

Maya writing consists of neat rows of hieroglyphs with complicated faces, animal forms, and abstract elements. A glyph, or glyph-group, fits into a square. Almost always, the glyphs are read in columns from top to bottom and in pairs from left to right. The glyphs consist of main signs (the major element in the glyph) and affixes (the minor element added to the side or top or bottom of the main sign), although sometimes a main sign will become an affix or an affix will be used as a main sign. Most glyphs are used as compounds—that is, they consist of a main sign and one or more affixes. Some glyphs have both a geometric or symbolic form and a variant form in the shape of a head that has human or animal characteristics. Estimates vary as to the number of main signs and affixes, but the currently authoritative catalogue of glyphs, compiled and published by archaeologist J. Eric S. Thompson, lists 492 main signs and 370 affixes. This list, however, includes some duplications of main signs and affixes, and it is also possible that some of the glyphs listed separately are actually variations of the same glyph. There is a general unity of glyphs throughout the whole Central area, but styles vary at different times. For example, early glyphs are more ornate than later ones and certain conventions were introduced in later times. One of the reasons for believing that the Dresden Codex is a copy of a Classic manuscript is that it combines early and late glyph styles.

The semantic structure of Maya writing is still a subject of debate. Some scientists believe that the writing was phonetic—that is, that the glyphs symbolize a syllable or sound, or at times perhaps only a single consonant. Others feel that the writing was essentially pictographic. They base their argument on the fact that a language that has as many glyphs as the Maya's is likely to be pictographic or ideographic in nature, because a phonetic language requires fewer symbols. For example, there are only twenty-six letters in the English alphabet, whereas there are some seven hundred Egyptian hieroglyphs. Another argument against the phonetic character of the language is the fact that different glyphs are used in different kinds of texts, and, if the language were truly phonetic, one would not expect such distinctions. However, increasing evidence for phoneticism has been accumulated in recent years, largely from the study of old dictionaries and recent Maya languages, and from the use of modern computers.

A number of glyphs have several meanings. The glyphs for days, for example, are also glyphs for gods, and sometimes they have other meanings as well. The glyph may denote the thing it pictures; it may denote a sound; and it may have other meanings derived from either of these (that is, it may have meanings no longer directly related to the original picture element, and it may also have rebus or pun meanings deriving from its sound in the manner of representing the English word "I" by the picture of an eye). Moreover, its meanings may change in context with other glyphs or affixes. One of the problems of decipherment is that the discovery of one meaning does not necessarily lead to all the meanings for that glyph, and another problem is that once one glyph is translated it does not necessarily help in translating others.

In deciphering language, one wants to know not only the meaning or meanings of a word, but how it was spoken, what it sounded like. The use of ancient dictionaries, the compilation of modern dictionaries, and the study of modern Maya languages have been productive ways of working, yielding not only possible interpretations for ancient words, but suggesting phonetic equivalents for glyphic elements which can be checked in various ways. In this kind of projecting back in time, the scholar must, of course, consider natural change in language and new words introduced from outside, but, if he finds the same root in several Maya languages, then it is probably fairly ancient. It is believed that the writers of ancient Maya spoke a language not very different from modern Maya languages. The sixteenth-century Motul dictionary, the seventeenth-century Vienna dictionary, and more recent ones have added to the knowledge of the ancient Maya languages, as has the *Chilam Balam*, the eighteenth- and nineteenth-century books of prophecy and lore of the Yucatec Maya. Although the *Books of Chilam Balam* are very late and written in Roman script, some of their material may well have been handed down from Classic Maya hieroglyphic texts.

Bishop Landa's *Relación de las Cosas de Yucatán* was the basic early source for a start on the study of Maya hieroglyphs. Brasseur de Bourbourg found Landa's *Relación* (at least part of it; the manuscript is still incomplete) and published it in 1864. Since that time scholars have been working to decipher the Maya glyphs, for in addition to an account of the history and mores of the Yucatec Maya, Landa also wrote down the meanings of a number of glyphs. His primary informant was a member of the Cocom family, a Maya prince who had been educated in the mysteries of writing, a knowledge that in pre-Conquest days was confined to the priests and the nobility. Landa did not list all the glyphs, and furthermore he noted that "already they do not use all these characters of theirs, especially the young people who have learned ours."

Dr. Linton Satterthwaite, Maya archaeologist, and an assistant at Tikal, with the oldest Maya stela yet found. The date, following the Initial Series glyph, reads 8.12.14.8.15, or A.D. 292.

Landa included the glyphs for days and months as well as an alphabet of Maya glyphs. The latter has been a source of much debate, for some authorities feel that Landa attempted to get an alphabet from his informants without realizing that the hieroglyphs might not be alphabetical, and even if Maya is largely phonetic, this still does not necessarily imply the existence of an alphabet of single letters. Landa's alphabet, however, is useful in giving a number of sounds and meanings.

It is ironic that Bishop Landa, who wrote down the only important guide to deciphering the glyphs, was also single-handedly responsible for the loss of a large number of Maya books that might have been enormously helpful in deciphering the language. He apparently found many ancient practices still surviving in Spanish Yucatán, among them the sacrifice of children who were baptized Christians, and was driven by his moral scruples to destroy the source of the ancient lore. Landa himself wrote:

> These people also made use of certain characters or letters, with which they wrote in their books their ancient affairs and sciences, and with these and drawings and with certain signs in these drawings, they understood their affairs and made others understand them and taught them. We found a great number of books in these characters, and, as they contained nothing in which there was not to be seen superstition and lies of the devil, we burned them all, which they regretted to an amazing degree and which caused them affliction.

The Church felt that Landa had overstepped his authority in perpetrating the auto-da-fé, and he was called back to Spain to justify his acts. It was while he was there that he wrote his *Relación*, which has to some extent made up to scholars for the loss of the Maya books.

Only four pre-Conquest Maya codices are known today. The largest of these folding-screen books is twenty-four feet long. Both sides of the screen-fold sheet were used, each fold forming a page, each of which was eight or nine inches high and three to five inches wide. The pages were read from left to right to the end of the sheet, and then back again from left to right on the other side. The Dresden Codex was found in Vienna in 1739; it is now in the State Library at Dresden, from which it takes its name. It is essentially a treatise on astronomy and divination, with tables of eclipse dates and revolutions of the plant Venus, divinatory almanacs, and information on ceremonies. The Codex Tro-Cortesianus, or Madrid Codex, was found in two pieces; one section belonged to a Spaniard named Tro, and the other section was called the Codex Cortesianus because it was said to have been brought across the Atlantic by Cortés. The halves are now united in Madrid. It is a book of horoscopes, which the priests used in making their divinations. The Paris, or Perez, Codex, was found in 1860 in the Bibliothèque Nationale in Paris, where it remains, and is only a fragment. It is involved with deities and ceremonies on one side and with divination on the other. The fourth codex, an eleven-page fragment with Venus tables, was found recently and is still questioned by some scholars. Known as the Grolier Codex, because it was first exhibited in the Grolier Club, it is now in the National Museum of Anthropology in Mexico. There were surely many other codices, but none is known to have survived the rain forest or Bishop Landa's auto-da-fé.

A newly realized source of Maya inscriptions is the now fairly large corpus of Maya vases, with scenes and inscriptions carved and painted on them. For a long time, few of these vases were widely known, and it was thought that most of their texts were meaningless. But it has now been ascertained that more or less the same inscription appears on most vases. Called the "Primary Standard Sequence," it is unique to vases, containing glyphs that are known elsewhere, but that do not appear elsewhere in this combination or sequence. The number of glyphs varies from vase to vase, but they tend to appear in a regular sequence even when some are omitted. The sequence seems to be a sort of hymn about the descent into the underworld.

The stone monuments, the most important source of texts, have been shown by studies in the last twenty years to be inscribed to a great extent with historical material. Their texts, particularly those of the stelae, normally begin with the date of dedication of the monument at the end of a twenty-year period—or a half or a quarter of this period. These dates refer back to the year the Maya or their predecessors selected as the beginning of the calendar or the beginning of the present creation of the world, an imaginary starting point for their system, the year 3133 B.C., a concept like our use of the beginning of the Christian era for our date system. The Maya believed that the world had been created a number of times—at least four, possibly more—and that each time it had been violently destroyed. The starting point of the present creation was probably established in Olmec times. The use of the calendar itself perhaps originated about 500 B.C. in Oaxaca or Veracruz.

The Maya not only dated their monuments, they sometimes calculated dates far beyond the beginning of their calendar, counting millions of years back into former creations of the world. These dates seem to mark the births of mythical ancestors of the kings whose histories are recorded on the monuments; they probably have ritual and astrological significance as well. The Maya did not differentiate between astronomy and astrology, between history and myth.

The Maya calendar is made up of a number of serial elements which, although simple in themselves, are complicated in the way they mesh. There are twenty Maya days, each of which is named and whose glyphs we can identify. Each day is a god. Ahau, for instance, is not just the name of a day; it is also the sun god, and it is used as a title. Imix, another day, is the earth god. Kan is the corn god, or corn, and Cimi is the god of death. Each day had a definite character, auspicious or malevolent. In the set sequence of the twenty days, each day was accompanied by a number, running consecutively from 1 to 13. For instance, the progression might be 1 Imix, 2 Ik, 3 Akbal, etc., going to 13 Ben. Then the numbers start over while the twenty names continue. At the end of the twenty names, one starts again with the names while the numbers continue. The continuation read 8 Imix, 9 Ik, 10 Akbal, etc. In this way, 260 days—13 times 20—pass before the same name is again accompanied by the same number, that is, before 1 and Imix are again paired.

This cycle of 260 days comprised the sacred calendar of the Maya. It is called the *tzolkin* or the Sacred Round or Almanac Year. The earliest evidence for this kind of calendar comes from outside the Maya area, from Monte Albán in Oaxaca in the Middle Pre-Classic period. It is quite possible, however, that the calendar originated in the Maya Lowlands. The arguments for this are based on the fact that writing and calendrics were more highly developed in the Maya Lowlands and that a number of the animals which give their names and faces to days—crocodile, jaguar, monkey, and iguana—are indigenous to the Lowlands but not to the Mexican plateau or the Maya Highlands.

The Maya also needed a secular calender. For this purpose they used the approximate solar year of 365 days, which they divided into eighteen "months" of twenty days each, with a year-end period, or "month," of five "dead" days. The days in the months are numbered 0 Pop, 1 Pop, etc., through 19 Pop, when one then goes on to the next month. Although it was a secular calendar, the months were also gods, as were the days. (There was actually no "0" day, but since the Maya counted elapsed time, this has come to be a convenient way of expressing the idea that o Pop was the beginning of the sequence of Pop days, a day that belonged to Pop, but had not yet become past time.)

These two calendars, the sacred and secular, mesh so that, for instance, a simple Maya date might read 1 Imix, 19 Pop, giving both the name of the day and the name of the month, each always accompanied by a number. It is a little as if we were to think concurrently of the daily calendar and the liturgical calendar, and were to say "the Third Sunday in Advent," followed by the calendar date. The two Maya calendars together do not repeat the same coincidence of dates for fifty-two years, and this cycle is known as the Calendar Round. The difficulty with a date of this kind is that every fifty-two years it is repeated. It is as if we were to write a date July 7, '65; we could know the place of the date within the century, but we would not know *which* century.

The Calendar Round was also used in other parts of Mesoamerica, and may well have been universal there in pre-Conquest times. The Aztec, for example, used a similar calendar and scholars have been able to compare its use of day names with those on the Maya calendar. The Calendar Round, however, was obviously inadequate for the Maya, who felt a need to count time in long periods. The "Long Count" method of measuring time, which seems to have been invented in the pre-Maya, post-Olmec period, described larger units of time in multiples of twenty; this vigesimal system was widely used by the Lowland Maya. (The earliest dates found in the Lowlands are Long Count dates from Tikal and Uaxactún at the beginning of the Classic period. These cities in the heart of the Petén also produced the earliest Classic sculpture and ceramic styles.) Time was measured in terms of *uinals* (months), a 20-day period; *tuns* (years), a 360-day period (here the twenty-multiple system breaks down, as the multipliers are 18 and 20, giving a figure that comes close to the length of the solar year); *katuns*, a period of twenty tuns, or 7,200 days; and *baktuns*, a period of twenty *katuns*, or 144,000 days. These periods of time are a little like our years, centuries, and millennia. There were also larger measurements of time, continuing in multiples of twenty, but the terms above are those used in most Maya dates. The dates in the Long Count calendar ran in cycles of thirteen bactuns; presumably the Maya believed that after the completion of the thirteenth baktun the world would be destroyed, and with its new creation the count of time would begin again.

The inscription on a Classic Maya stela marking a katun ending begins with a Long Count date. The first glyph in the date is the Initial Series glyph. It is usually larger than the other glyphs in the inscription, and is always the same except for its central element, which is the glyph for the deity of the month in which the date terminates. Below it, the column of text begins with a pair of glyphs: to the left, the baktun glyph, to the right the katun glyph. Below these is another pair: the tun (or year) glyph to the left, the uinal (or month) glyph to the right. Below this, to the left, is the glyph counting the number of days; to the right is the glyph for the specific day. Below this, sometimes with other glyphs intervening, is the glyph for the specific month. Thus, the first five glyphs after the Initial Series glyph are a counting of time, and following these are two glyphs giving the date. Such a date might be translated into Arabic numerals as 9.15.0.0.0, 3 Ahau 3 Mol; that is, 9 baktuns, 15 katuns, 0 tuns, 0 months, and 0 days since the beginning of the calendar, the date falling on 3 Ahau 3 Mol. The number of months and days would always be 0 because the stelae were erected at the end of even periods of twenty years, although sometimes half- or even quarter-katuns were commemorated. Not all stelae have katun-ending dates. The earliest stela yet found, for example, has a date of 8.12.14.8.15, A.D. 292. Such stelae were obviously erected for some other commemorative purpose.

Initial Series, or Long Count, dates were one of the criteria of the Classic period, and the Classic period has sometimes been called the Initial Series period. Toward the end of the Classic period the use of Initial Series dating ceased, and the Period Ending method was used. In this case, only a glyph showing the end of the katun and the glyphs for the day and the month were needed. Still later, the Short Count was used, in which one glyph expressed the katun ending. These later dating methods gained in economy, but they lost in accuracy.

Although we can interpret Maya Long Count dates with perfect accuracy within the frame of reference of the Maya calendar, there is still some question about equating this calendar with our own. There are two major correlation systems, one called the Goodman-Martínez Hernández-Thompson system (usually shortened to Thompson correlation, or G-M-T correlation), the other the Spinden correlation, which places the dates about 260 years earlier. At first, systems of correlation were based chiefly on historical sources, and attempts were made to confirm the logic of their time span by examining ceramic material and art styles. However, part of the correlation difficulty has arisen because the historical sources, which are themselves late, do not agree, although in general they support

The back of a stela at Copán, with an inscription beginning with an Initial Series glyph.

the Thompson correlation. There have been attempts to confirm correlation by astronomical evidence, but this has led to varying, inconclusive results. Carbon-14 dates have been studied recently in connection with this problem. At first this method seemed to confirm the Spinden correlation, but the bulk of carbon-14 dates at this writing supports the Thompson correlation, which is generally accepted and is used as the basis of dates given in this book. Refinements should still perhaps be made.

Maya mathematics, like Maya calendrics, was based on a unit of twenty. One of the remarkable things about this system is that it was positional, as our decimal system is. When we write $10.00 or $00.01, we are using the same digits, but their position gives them different values. The same is true of the Maya system; the chief difference is that the Maya used multiples of twenty rather than ten. The numbers could be written either vertically or horizontally. Numbers were most commonly written in the bar-and-dot system of notation. A dot is 1; four dots is 4; a bar is 5; a bar and dot 6, two bars 10, three bars 15. However, instead of using four bars for 20, the figure is moved to the next position, so that a dot then equals one unit of 20. It is the same idea as our writing 20 as 2 and 0. The Maya, however, because their system was vigesimal—based on twenty—would write 1 (that is, one unit of twenty) and zero. Thus the bars and dots, according to their position, indicate digits, twenties, four hundreds (twenty times twenty), eight thousands (twenty times four hundred), etc. A count back in time could be made very rapidly with this progression. Bar-and-dot numbers appear frequently in Maya inscriptions. For example, at the beginning of a stela inscription a bar-and-dot numeral ordinarily accompanies the glyphs for the baktun and katun, and a zero normally appears beside the glyphs for the counts of the years, months, and days.

The flexibility and subtlety of Maya arithmetical notation is striking when compared with the clumsy Roman numeral system that was being used in Europe at the time. Neither ancient Greece nor Rome had either a positional system or a concept of zero. In fact, zero was not known in Europe until after the end of the Classic Maya period, when Europe was introduced to the Arabic numeral system. The Maya cipher for zero was usually a conventionalized shell, which was used in their positional system just as we use our zero.

The bar-and-dot system of enumeration was used in Pre-Classic times by the inhabitants of southern Veracruz and Oaxaca. The interpretation of its use by the Maya comes to us from the *Chilam Balam*.

Personification is constantly found in Maya mathematics and calendrics, and there are also Maya glyphs in the form of human heads for numbers from 1 to 19. And not only the days had characters; so did the numbers, or the gods of the numbers. They were favorable or unfavorable: the gods of 4, 7, 9, and 13 were benevolent; those of 2, 3, 5, and 10 were malevolent.

The Maya were extraordinary astronomers, and the date inscriptions on the stelae were often followed by astronomical data. It is no easy feat to make observations of sunrises and sunsets, eclipses, the movements of Venus, etc., in a country where it rains for nearly nine months of the year. It is also remarkable that the Maya were able to make astronomical observations with such minimal equipment. A pair of crossed sticks was set up inside the temple—perhaps this was a reason for building temples on top of high pyramids—as a fixed position from which another fixed position on the horizon (some natural object) could be seen. Observations were made as the sun, moon, or planets repeated their movements in reference to these fixed points. The Maya must have collected data over a long period of time as a base for their calculations, and they quite possibly inherited the observations of earlier people, such as the Olmec. One must remember that the Maya had no concept of a round earth. The movements of heavenly bodies were not thought of as revolutions but as events that repeated themselves in a given pattern, as time itself was a repeating pattern.

It is generally agreed that the moon was carefully observed by the Maya. Most of the Initial Series dates on monuments include glyphs that indicate the current age of the moon and other data about its position and time relationship. This Lunar Series often appears between the glyphs for the day and the month, so it was obviously of primary importance. In the Late Classic period there was evidently a uniform method of counting moons that was used in virtually all the Lowland sites. Eight pages of the Dresden Codex are devoted to lunar tables that predict solar eclipses, and it also includes five pages of tables devoted to the planet Venus. Venus makes one revolution in approximately 584 days. It appears as the Morning Star for approximately 240 days; it disappears for about 90 days; it reappears as the Evening Star for another 240 days; and then it disappears again for 14 days before appearing as the Morning Star again. The number of days in the total revolution was important to the Maya because it could be synchronized with the year of 365 days and the sacred almanac of 260 days. At the end of two Calendar Rounds, there

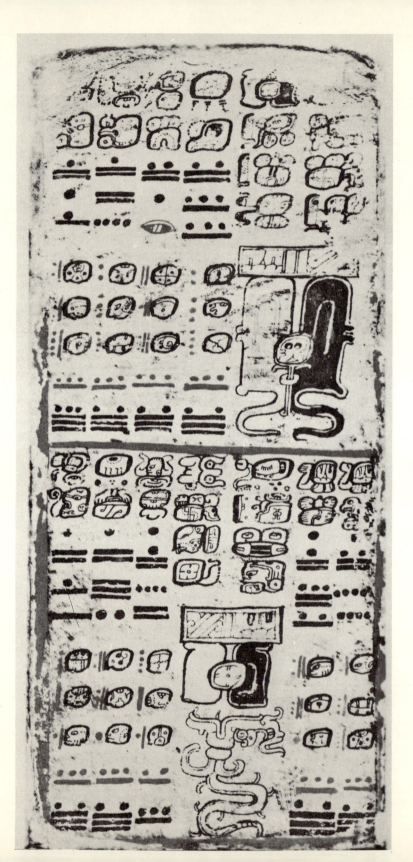

will have been 65 revolutions of Venus, 104 years of 365 days, and 146 cycles of the sacred 260-day calendar. The Maya may also have been aware of the movements of Saturn, Jupiter, and Mercury; these cycles may have been synchronized with the others. The problem of the correction of the difference between the solar year of 365.2422 days and the Maya year of 365 days long puzzled investigators, but it is now believed that this was achieved, not through solar calculations, but through lunar counts.

The Maya penchant for working out parallel calculations and then meshing them should now be apparent. Other astronomical and ritualistic calculations also provided strands that could be woven into this same pattern. There was, for example, a cycle of 819 days, based on numbers that had ritual importance because of the deities they represented. The Maya calendar became increasingly complex as additional significant cycles were added and higher numbers became the common denominator of these cycles.

For the Maya, astronomy and astrology were not really separated, since the science of observation and prediction was closely interwoven with divination and the relationship between the real world and the sacred one. Scientists were undoubtedly priests, and science was the mysterious lore of the priests. The priests' arcane astronomical knowledge gave them power. When a priest predicted an eclipse and the eclipse came about on schedule, the ignorant peasant must indeed have been impressed with the priest's supernatural powers and this evidence of his liaison with the deities. Another important facet of these calculations was divination, for favorable and unfavorable times were predicted by the priests through these tables. It is as if all the secrets of the universe were to be found through these calculations, and the lives of the Maya people must have been rigidly adjusted to the calendar and its portents. It is not surprising that the Maya were fatalistic.

The Maya left their hieroglyphs on virtually everything they touched: Maya sculpture is almost always engraved with long texts, and there must once have been a great many books. Glyphs are also found on a number of small objects, including those made of jade, shell, obsidian, and bone. Carved glyphs vary in style from painted ones. Glyphs carved on small objects are the same as those found on sculptured monuments, and they are often calendrical.

In the past, studies relating to the calendar and mathematics dominated much of the work on Maya hieroglyphs, for calendrical and

Eclipse table from the Dresden Codex.

Carved onyx bowl with glyphs around the rim and a figure holding a ceremonial bar with a glyph headdress.

astronomical calculations make up much of the content of the texts, and also it was somewhat easier to get a foothold on the study of the number glyphs than on some of the more subtle aspects of the language. The calendrical glyphs, it should be said, have been much better understood than the astronomical ones. Recent work in decipherment has dealt more with histories—with genealogies and accession to power—than it did a few years ago. Other facets of the current work deal with the structure of the language, its clauses and parts of speech—for example, names, titles, and glyphs for actions can now be spotted.

The language is being studied by archaeologists and anthropologists who are specialists in the area, and by linguists who are specialists in language systems in general. Other scholars with varying backgrounds— for example, cryptographers, artists, iconographers who relate glyphs to ritual objects and costumes, and people with knowledge of natural history who can recognize what animals or plants some glyphs may have derived from—all have joined in multidisciplinary work to attack the knotty problems of the language. New sources of inscriptions are available, and there are new ideas and techniques to work with. Computers, for example, have been used to determine frequencies, contexts, and probabilities.

Further progress with the glyphs tells us more about the Maya in general. Work on the historical parts of the texts is beginning to reveal likely knowledge about political structure, the relationships between centers, their military alliances, what "king" married what "princess," and who conquered whom. Work on parts of texts that seem to have to do with gods and rituals can give insight into religion and social structure.

In the last few years, remarkable strides have been made, and it may not be long before much of the writing can be read with comparative ease. Each year brings new developments and new successes in the detective work on decipherment and on the background in which it developed. It may not be long before the complete texts can be read as a language— possibly even a pronounceable one.

VII.
RELIGION

The cosmological beliefs of the Classic Maya are not fully known, for the only direct source of knowledge lies in the sculptured and painted representations of deities and ceremonies. The concept of the Maya cosmos must be reconstructed from these, with the help of later legends and cosmologies that may be related to the beliefs of the Classic period. An Aztec belief that the world rested on the back of a gigantic alligator in the middle of an enormous pond can probably be found also in Maya thought. Many religious and cosmological beliefs were shared throughout Mesoamerica. A variant concept is that the Maya thought of the earth as the floor of a house of gigantic iguanas which reached to the zenith.

The Maya cosmos was complex. It seems to have been made up of thirteen heavens, or thirteen compartments of heaven, in which thirteen sky deities resided. These deities were most likely the gods of the thirteen day numbers of the sacred calendar. There were also nine underworlds ruled by the nine lords of the night, whose glyphs appear in calendrical inscriptions, often interrupting the calendrical text. A giant tree rose up through the center of this structure, its roots in the underworld, its branches in heaven. There was apparently warfare between the sky gods and those of the underworld. (The numbers nine and thirteen were ritually significant to the Maya, and are factors in the count of the 819-

day calendrical cycle.) Maya deities, however, had a disquieting way of not remaining in one realm or another, and the same deity often appears both in the sky and in the underworld. The sun god, for example, his glyph accompanied by different attributes, appears in inscriptions as one of the lords of the night, for the sun god was believed to have gone to the underworld at sunset. In addition to the gods of the sky and the underworld, there may also have been a group of seven deities associated with the surface of the earth.

Maya deities generally are related to the forces of nature; perhaps some should be thought of not as gods but as personifications of these forces, which were critical to agriculture. The everyday life of the peasant centered around the rain, sun, and wind gods, who were—and still are—invoked when the fields are cut, burned, and planted, and while the crop is growing. As the society grew more complex, the religious pantheon also grew more complicated, with new gods being added, old gods taking on new functions, and the whole array becoming more esoteric. Maya deities are sometimes extremely elusive, and it is difficult indeed to reconstruct all the functions of all of them. Most of them seem to have had a dual nature, and could be either beneficent or malevolent. The malevolent nature of a god was often expressed in painting or sculpture by the addition of a death sign. The gods who brought rain for the crops were the same gods who sent damaging hail and excessive dampness. They granted beneficence in exchange for offerings and prayers, and the ceremonies grew more complicated as the religion developed. Also, the priestly necessity to explain natural phenomena increased the complexity of the deities themselves.

Not only could Maya gods change their place and their function and the goodness or evil of their nature, they could also change form; the same deity might appear as young or old, and sometimes deities even seem to have changed sex. The gods varied in importance from place to place and from time to time. Sometimes they were known by different names; sometimes the same god had different attributes in different situations.

At the time of the Conquest, Itzamná, a sky god, was the most important Maya god in Yucatán, and he was probably extremely important at all periods, for he is frequently depicted in Classic art. In the codices, Itzamná is represented as an old man but at other times he appears as a celestial monster—a lizard-like creature, often with two

Carved black pottery vase showing the god known as GI of the Palenque Triad. This vase, decorated with red cinnabar, comes from southern Yucatán.

heads, one of which is that of an old man. He was the lord of the heavens as well as the lord of day and night, and was at times a terrestrial monster. *Itzam* means a large water lizard, and *na* is "house"—hence, the "lizard house" of Maya cosmology. The Maya tended to depict rain or water gods with reptilian characteristics. The deities often have animal or plant origins mixed with human attributes; purely human forms are rare in the symbolic representations of Maya art. Itzamná was not only reptilian and associated with nature, but was also a sort of creator god and a culture hero who was credited with the invention of writing. Itzamná seems to have been always benevolent.

Itzamná is sometimes identified with Kinich Ahau, the sun god, and they may possibly have been different aspects of the same deity, although they often seem quite separate and one will have greater importance in some places than the other. Kinich Ahau, a great hunter and the patron of art and music, was one of the gods most frequently represented in Classic times in the Central area. In the sites of the Puuc region and in northern Yucatán generally, Chac, the rain god, was more frequently represented on Classic-period sculpture. In the northern area there is less rainfall than in the southern Petén, and drought was sometimes a serious problem, so it is logical that the sun god should be more important in the rain forest and the rain god in the drier areas of Yucatán. The rain god may also be another manifestation of Itzamná, the general sky god.

Some deities could be both one god and four; there were four Itzamnás, for example, one on each side of the world. There was one rain god, Chac, but there were also four Chacs. There was a wind god, yet wind gods also appeared at the four sides of the world. This idea is somewhat analogous to that of the Christian Trinity. With the Maya penchant for parallel mathematical sequences, it was not out of character for them to have gods who were simultaneously one and four. Four Bacabs, or sky-bearers, also stood at each of the four sides of the world to hold up the sky. Four gods called Pauahtuns held up the earth. Each world direction was associated with a color: red for the east, white for the north, black for the west, and yellow for the south. Bacabs, Pauahtuns, and rain and wind gods were also identified with these world-direction colors. (Color was of ritual importance to the Maya. They associated colors with days. On ceremonial occasions they painted their bodies.) At each of the four cardinal points stood a sacred tree, a "tree of abundance," from which man's first food came. There was also a fifth tree rising to heaven from the center of the world. These trees, which are associated with the rain gods, are represented in Classic sculpture. Stylized crosslike versions of the trees were found by the Spaniards at the time of the Conquest, when the Yucatec Maya prayed to the trees for rain, and they are still to be found today in the Maya area, although their symbolism has mingled with that of the Christian cross. These tree-crosses are painted green and referred to as "our Lord Santa Cruz."

A deity who is associated with the north and the North Star can also be connected with all four points of the compass and appears, in another

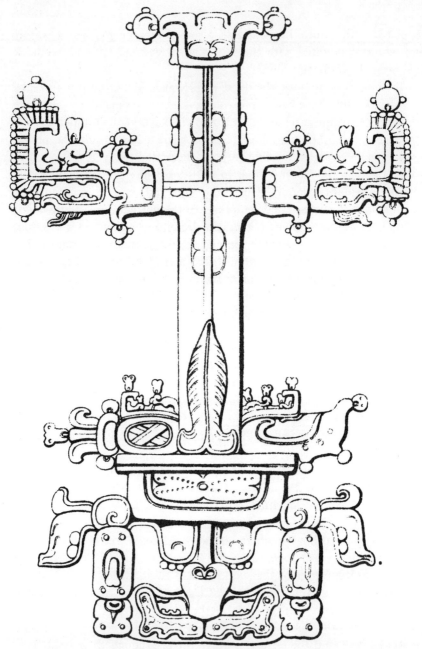

DRAWING BY A. P. MAUDSLAY

A Maya "cross," from a sculpture at Palenque.

context, as one of the lords of the night. Not only did the Maya believe that gods could be both one and four, but they were also considered the thirteen gods of the sky, or the upper world, and the nine gods of the underworld as a single collective deity.

In 1904, in an attempt to unravel some of the problems of identification of Maya deities, Paul Schellhas listed the attributes of the deities in the Maya manuscripts and designated them by the noncommittal terminology of Gods A, B, C, etc. It has become evident that Schellhas's catalogue is not comprehensive enough to take in all the aspects of Maya deities, but his designations are still used and useful.

God A is a death god, whose head is a skull and whose ribs are bare bone; his cheek is often marked with a design like a percentage sign. God B, the long-nosed or long-lipped god, is now generally considered to be Chac, the rain god. God C, also a sky god, has a stylized monkey face. God D is now thought to be Itzamná. God E is the maize god, who was probably also a general agricultural deity. He is pictured as youthful and handsome, and usually has a maize plant sprouting from his cleft. God F is associated with war and human sacrifice. God G is the sun god, also known as Kinich Ahau. God H is probably another rain god, as well as the god of the number nine and of the day Chicchan.

There were two goddesses—I and O—who have frequently been confused in terms of their associations with the moon, weaving, medicine, childbirth, rain, licentiousness, and fertility. In the Post-Classic period, on the east coast of the Yucatán peninsula, there was an important cult of the goddess Ixchel, who must have been one of these deities. She was a moon goddess, and, as such, was probably the wife of the sun god, either Kinich Ahau or Itzamná in the aspect of the sun god.

God K was described by Schellhas as "The God with the Ornamented Nose." It has become clear in more recent studies that it is not the nose but the brow that is ornamented, and that the ornament is actually a smoking cigar sticking out from a mirror in the brow of the god. This god seems to have a good deal to do with the accession to power of Maya kings. His head is frequently depicted at the ends of the ceremonial bars that are held by figures on monuments, and he is depicted on "manikin scepters"—other regal objects comparable to the scepters of modern kings. One of God K's attributes is a leg that ends in a serpent head. It is now thought that this god is to be identified with the later Aztec god Tezcatlipoca, "Smoking Mirror," who also had a snake foot.

The Destruction of the World by Flood, from the Dresden Codex. The reptile at the top of the picture is Itzamná. The woman with the upturned bowl is probably Goddess O. The figure at the bottom is the black God L with a bird on his head.

God L is an important death-associated god, an old man with a black face and a toothless mouth. He wears a malevolent-looking bird, usually on a large hat. He was surely one of the major gods of the underworld. God M, also black-faced (Maya warriors painted themselves black for war), may carry spears and wear a bundle on his back, which some scholars have thought to be a merchant's pack. God N is one of the most frequently depicted deities. He, too, is an old god, and surely the principal earth god, although he often wears a bit of fishnet in his headdress and is usually distinguished by a shell—he may be coming out of the shell or holding it, and it may be any of a number of types of shells. He may have been Pauahtun, the god who held up the earth. In Maya thought, earth and water were conceived of as complementary, not contradictory, as were day and night, and life and death. God P, the last in Schellhas's series, was a frog-headed god of rare appearance.

Schellhas tabulated the appearances of the gods in the codices, and found God B (the rain god) most frequently depicted; second, with about half the number of appearances, was God D (Itzamná, the sky god); God E (the maize or agricultural deity) was third, appearing almost as many times as God D. Considering that the codices deal in large part with celestial phenomena and agricultural rites, this representation is not surprising. It is interesting, however, that on the monuments God K, the regal symbol, is undoubtedly most frequently seen, and on vases it is probably God N, the earth and underworld god, who is most common, with God L, another underworld god, a close second. The frequent appearance of underworld gods on the vases is evidence for the argument that the vases depict scenes in the underworld and were made especially as grave goods.

The gods described above do not complete the list of representations in Maya art that have been called deities. A god who was apparently imported in later times was Kulkulkán, the deity known in the Aztec-speaking world as Quetzalcóatl, the "feathered serpent," an ancient god in Mesoamerica, but one that did not appear in Classic Maya art. Kulkulkán and Quetzalcóatl were associated with the planet Venus, whose movements were considered very important by the Maya. There had to have been a Classic-period Venus god. The *Popol Vuh* tells of two brothers, Xbalanque and Hunapu, who, after various adventures, overcame the lords of the underworld, and became celestial bodies. Xbalanque became the sun (or God G, or Kinich Ahau) and Hunapu became Venus.

Hunapu may also have been a god known as GI, who appears in the Classic period.

Gods GI, GII, and GIII are known as the Palenque Triad—they are found at that site, in sequence, on inscriptions—although they also appear elsewhere. GI is characterized by a shell ear-ornament and diadem, a Roman nose, and an odd tooth. Kings at Palenque and Copán may appear in the guise of GI. GII is probably to be identified with God K. The glyph for GII is usually a supine figure, with its knees tucked up and the head of God K. Kings of Palenque may also appear as God K. GIII, who has jaguar characteristics, is the night-sun lord of the underworld.

Each god was accompanied by a complex of associations. In addition to representing forces of nature, they were known in Post-Classic times to have been the patrons of merchants, tattooers, hunters, fishermen, comedians, dancers, singers, poets, and many other occupations. Bacab, for example, was the patron deity of beekeepers. At the time of the Conquest these patron aspects of many deities were dominant.

There were animal deities as well, and periods of time also appeared as gods, which is hardly surprising, considering the Maya obsession with the calendar. The days were gods, the numbers accompanying them were gods, and the larger periods of time were also deities.

Knowledge of the pantheon as a whole is sketchy; more is understood about attributes and contexts than about the real nature of these beings and how they were regarded. The only direct sources of information are the artifacts of the Classic period. Early Spanish writers are useful, if prejudiced, but by the sixteenth century other gods and other rituals had been introduced from Central Mexico, and even the gods who had remained from Classic times had changed emphasis and function with the breakdown of the theocratic society. Even the Maya codices are late, although they are one of the most important sources on the deities, for they contain material that had surely been handed down for generations, and they give portraits of deities recognizable in earlier sources. Recent investigations show a tendency of religious and cosmological ideas to be, in some degree, pan-Mesoamerican, so Maya concepts can be compared—cautiously—with those from other times and places.

The Maya believed in an afterlife. The Post-Classic Maya thought that warriors killed in battle, sacrificed victims, women who died in childbirth, and those who had committed suicide by hanging went directly to paradise. The Maya paradise was apparently a place of peace and plenty where one could rest eternally under the shade of the sacred tree. Those who had been evil in this world went to an unpleasant under-

Polychrome vase showing God N, the old god, or earth god, seated in a conch shell. Six and a quarter inches high.

A page from the Codex Tro-Cortesianus, or Madrid Codex, showing the world directions with the sacred tree in the center. At

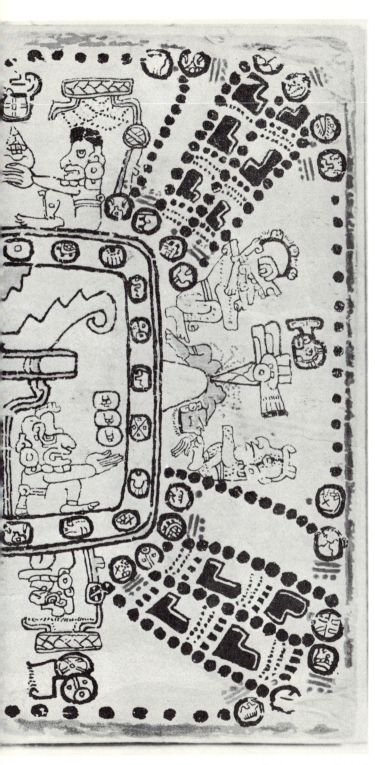

the right is a scene of human sacrifice, with the victim flanked
by the death god and the god associated with human sacrifice.

world. In Yucatán there is a belief that those who have done evil on earth return in the bodies of animals or human beings, or as an evil wind.

Maya life must have consisted of one religious ceremony after another. The principal functions of the priests were to propitiate the gods, to be the guardians of the astronomical and calendrical data, and to tell the people when to cut and burn their fields, when to plant, and—surely one of their most important duties—when to celebrate religious rites.

Before a ceremony the priests and others who were to take part observed a period of fasting and celibacy to symbolize a purity of spirit with which they would go through the ritual. At the ceremony copal was burned, prayers and ritual dances performed, and an offering made. Sometimes animals were offered for sacrifice, or gifts of food, feathers, and precious stones were made to the gods. Ordinarily, when prayers were made for rain, good crops, or good hunting or fishing, the priests and people drew blood from their ears, lips or tongues as an offering to strengthen the prayers. Bloodletting is also depicted on Classic-period monuments and pottery as part of a rite of purification and humiliation engaged in by the king as a means of achieving power.

At some ceremonies human sacrifice was required, but usually only in times of dire calamity, such as drought and famine, or during the severe illness of a ruler. There are a few scenes of human sacrifice in the art of the Classic period, but the large-scale human sacrifice that the Spaniards found in the sixteenth century was surely the result of other influences and was based on the concept that the gods needed the nourishment of large amounts of human blood to sustain themselves and in order to continue giving sun and rain and fertility to mankind.

The strong element of idolatry found by the Spanish conquerors is also generally assumed to have been introduced by less civilized people who came into the area after the decline of the Classic period. From the artifacts, it seems clear that the Classic Maya did not worship images in a simple or literal sense. There are very few objects that represent a single deity. Usually representations of deities and their symbols are woven into the complicated pattern of the historical and ritual record that makes up the texts found on the sculpture. Maya religion is so intricately interwoven with the calendrical and astronomical calculations that played such an important part in Maya intellectual life that it is often hard to draw the line between the mathematical calculations and the significance of the deities themselves.

A page from the Dresden Codex, showing part of the Year-Bearers' ceremonies. At the bottom the god Itzamná carries a decapitated bird to the sacred tree, which rests on a year glyph. In the center sits God A, the death god, with a "percentage" sign on his cheek and skull-and-crossbones on his garment. At the top a Bacab carries a death god, the burden of the New Year.

Confirmation of this lies in the ceremonies that were held regularly in connection with the calendar. The ritual that marked the fulfillment of a katun cycle must have been one of the most impressive. When the cache offering was placed and the new stela raised, large numbers of people undoubtedly crowded into the ceremonial centers to participate in a colorful ceremony with ritual paraphernalia. Each katun had its special deity and special rites. According to Landa, the idol of the deity of the katun ruled in the temple for the first ten years of the katun and then, for the second half of the katun, the idol shared the temple with the idol of the succeeding katun, who then ruled alone for the first half of his own katun.

The ritual that is best known today is the New Year, or Year-Bearer's, celebration because it is still perpetuated in some remote areas. Also, both the Dresden and the Madrid Codices include representations of these ceremonies, and Bishop Landa and other sixteenth-century sources provide information regarding them. The first day of the month Pop was the New Year's or Year-Bearer's day. Because of the way the months and days of the Maya calendar synchronize, this first day of Pop could fall on only four day names, each of which was associated with a world-direction and a color. Because these days prophesied the fortunes of the coming year, the New Year was one of the most important times in the Maya calendar.

According to Bishop Landa, each town in Yucatán had two facing piles of stone at each of the four entrances of the town, which marked the four world directions, or cardinal points. At the time of the New Year ceremonies the image of the new god, with the appropriate color, was placed on the heap facing the image of the god who had ruled for the previous four years. There were then various rituals and processions, and the image of the god was censed with copal resin ground with maize. A bird was sacrificed by decapitation, and the idol was then placed on a frame representing one of the world-direction trees. This was followed by other processions, dances, and rituals. In the twentieth century, in the areas where the Year-Bearer's ceremony is still celebrated, a period of abstinence is observed by those participating in the ceremonies. A chicken or turkey—the choice depends on the wealth of the participants —is decapitated, tree branches are cut and tied to a cross, and beeswax candles are burned in front of the church door. The ceremony has become inextricably merged with Christian symbols, but its roots are firmly planted in the Maya past.

VIII.
THE END OF
MAYA SPLENDOR

The disappearance of the Central Classic Maya culture, which died within a century, is one of the great mysteries of archaeology. The decline can be dated fairly precisely because it is known when the Maya stopped erecting stelae in each of the major centers. In A.D. 790 nineteen cities erected stelae. Copán's last hieroglyphic monument is dated 800, and several sites raised their last dated monuments in 810. Tikal's last stela dates from 869. By 889 only three sites raised stelae, and the last known Initial Series date is 909. Not only did the Maya cease to erect dated stelae, they stopped building in the centers. In some cases, platform supports were abandoned before the buildings were put on top of them or walls of new buildings were left unfinished. It is true that some buildings were constructed after the carving of stelae had ceased, but these are rare.

There are dozens of theories to explain why the Classic Maya cities were abandoned so abruptly. One theory offered by many scholars suggests that it was due at least in part to a peasant revolt. The proponents of this theory feel that the peasant class might have rebelled against the increasing demands of the priests and nobles to produce more food and build more temples, and that the priests might have been too remote from the people. Certainly the period just preceding the decline was the period of greatest artistic and architectural activity and probably the period of greatest priestly power. Recent evidence, however, seems to suggest that Maya society was less rigidly structured than was previously thought, and that the peasant may well have shared in the civic and ceremonial life of the center, as he does in certain remote parts of the Maya area today. Recent house-mound excavations also suggest that he shared in the general wealth of the society. If this is true, it was not likely that the peasant had cause for revolt and even had he found cause, he would probably have been well enough initiated into the civic and ritual life of the social structure to have perpetuated it under different leaders or in a different form.

Another reason for doubting that the end of the Maya civilization was due to a peasant revolt is that it seems strange that there was never any resurgence of the peasant class afterward. How can it be explained that the peasants did not replace the old society with a new one? In other areas of Mesoamerica—indeed, in other parts of the world—civilizations run their courses through cycles and declines, but there is always a new civilization to replace the old and begin over again, and tradition was strong in the Maya. In their working methods, art, social structure, and way of life generally, they were conservative people. If the Maya decline were simply a matter of revolt, it would seem that, even allowing for the clean broom of revolution, the traditions, although possibly transformed, would have been perpetuated in some way. For example, one would expect the small centers to have continued functioning even after the major centers were abandoned. It is the abruptness of the cessation of all civic activity that is strange. The revolt theory, for these reasons, seems unsatisfactory as a single cause of decline, although overextension of the power of the noble and priestly class may well have been part of the collapse equation.

There is still a more important argument against the theory of revolt: the drastic decrease in population on all social levels. Throughout the Late Classic period the Central area was one of the most densely settled parts of Mesoamerica and then, within a hundred years, most of this population vanished. Since the tenth century the Central area has been one of the most sparsely populated parts of Mesoamerica. There is considerable archaeological evidence pointing to a Post-Classic population decline: a lack of Post-Classic pottery (whereas there is a great deal of pottery from the Pre-Classic and Classic periods); a scarcity of Post-Classic house mounds; and, in general, a shortage of artifacts datable after A.D. 900. There is little evidence of any considerable Post-Classic population in the heart of the Central area except around Lake Petén

Itzá, which is still the most populous part of the northern Petén. A new society would have needed a peasant class from which to evolve, and apparently the peasant class itself was seriously depopulated. To understand the decline of the civilization, one must understand the decline of the population, and this remains shrouded in mystery.

Disease has been suggested as a possible cause for depopulation and disruption of the society, although no evidence of any fatal epidemic has yet been discovered. The great killers of the sixteenth century were malaria, smallpox, measles, and whooping cough—all introduced by the Spaniards. There is no evidence of pre-Conquest mass burials that would indicate a serious epidemic, nor has any clue to serious disease been found in skeletal material. Some scholars have suggested the possibility that nutritional problems were a cause of population decline, but this has not yet been proven.

Earthquake has also been mentioned as a causative catastrophe, but there is no geological evidence of earthquakes violent or widespread enough to have caused the decline of the whole area. It has also been suggested that drastic climatic changes and severe fluctuations of rainfall caused erosion and crop failure, but here again there is no real evidence. A long period of drought or of heavy rainfall might have been a factor in upsetting the ecology and economy of the Maya, but a geological-biological study made of a swamp near Tikal clearly indicates that there has been no major climatic change in the last eleven thousand years.

Many of the studies involving the problem of Maya decline have centered around ecology and agriculture. There were arguments that the growing population of the Central area could not have been supported by slash-and-burn farming, because the pressure of increased population would have caused the slash-and-burn cycle to be shortened, lessening the yield of each planting, preventing the forest from developing sufficiently to choke out the weed growth, and leading eventually to savannization, in which grassy plants would take over the forest and make the land unusable for crops. However, studies have indicated that many savannas are ancient, and would, therefore, have been a part of the environment, not a result of its use; moreover, the argument that the growing population of the Central area could not have been supported by slash-and-burn farming has been met by increasing evidence of other agricultural techniques. If these studies have not answered the question of the Maya decline, they have at least indicated that it is not likely that it was simply a matter of crop failure and malnutrition.

Some recent attempts to understand the decline have been based on economic factors. The Central Maya area lacked many goods that it needed to support its complex society and large population. Because of these needs, a long-distance trade system was built up with the Guatemalan and Chiapas Highlands (for obsidian and for hard stone for corngrinding), and probably also with the northern and western Yucatán peninsula (for salt). This argument asserts that the intermediate areas, through which this trade passed, must have gradually grown in power and gained control of the trade, thus weakening the power of the Central sites.

A number of recent studies have focused on what is now called the Middle Classic period, dating A.D. 400–700. The term refers chiefly to cities outside the Maya area. The Middle Classic saw the florescence and decline of Teotihuacán, in Central Mexico, and the flourishing of regional centers like Tajín (Central Veracruz), Xochicalco (Central Highlands), and sites in Oaxaca and the Pacific slopes of Guatemala. These sites surround the Maya area, and the dates of the Middle Classic period bracket the dates of the hiatus between the Maya Early and Late Classic periods. It is probably not accidental that between A.D. 550 and 600, when there was a virtual cessation of recorded activity in the Maya area, other places were suddenly blooming.

The Maya hiatus may have foreshadowed the end of the Classic Maya civilization, and there may be clues to the understanding of the Maya decline in a study of the Middle Classic period, when Teotihuacán was certainly the most influential city in Mesoamerica. In the Early Classic period, there was a clear influence from Teotihuacán on Maya art, which is especially noticeable at Tikal, where there is pottery made in a style imported from Teotihuacán, and four stelae with motifs identified with Teotihuacán. Many questions have been asked about this influence. What sort of relationship do these borrowings reflect? Were there actually artists from Teotihuacán at Tikal? Was the influence transmitted through Kaminaljuyú, in the Highland area, where the art is also affected by Teotihuacán, or was it direct? Did this artistic influence reflect a deeper tie with Teotihuacán? What did this relationship have to .do with the Maya hiatus, and did the hiatus relate to the decline of Teotihuacán? After the hiatus, the Teotihuacán influence vanished. Teotihuacán failed in A.D. 700, and between A.D. 700 and 900 the Maya cities reached their apogee, but the fall of Teotihuacán may have been the beginning of the end of the Maya.

Stela from Seibal, showing a mixture of Maya and non-Maya motifs. The hairdress, for example, is non-Maya.

Another factor that has been suggested to explain the collapse of the Central area is invasion and warfare with outsiders. Teotihuacán's demise was caused by less civilized peoples from the north, and there were also people moving on the edge of the Maya area in the Late Classic period. The Toltec people, in the Post-Classic period, moved from Central Mexico to the tip of the Yucatán peninsula and to the Guatemalan Highlands, and became the ruling class in both these areas, although they were Mayanized to some extent in the process—the Maya language is still used in these areas today.

The Northern area and the Guatemalan Highlands, where the Toltec settled, were not generally depopulated, as was the Central area. The invaders came in and settled with the existing population. Their history, although not absolutely clear, is certainly known in outline, but the impact of the Toltec people on the Central area and the part they may have played in the population decrease is still a mystery. In order to reach either Yucatán or the Highlands they would have had to pass along the periphery of the Central area, and in a few places in the Central area along the route they might have used there is evidence of violence: sculpture was defaced in a number of places, for example, and smashed thrones have been found at Piedras Negras. Yet there is no sign of large-scale destruction, and there is little evidence that they actually settled in the Central area—the natural environment probably did not appeal to them, as they would have preferred the Highlands or the dry tip of Yucatán—but there is evidence of their influence at certain sites along their route.

Recent clues about the decline of the Maya have been found on the southern edge of the Petén, where the Peabody Museum of Harvard University has been working at two sites, Seibal and Altar de Sacrificios. Altar de Sacrificios was one of the last Maya centers to erect a dated stela, in A.D. 889. The pottery shows strong outside influence during the last century of the Classic period at Altar, providing another demonstration that the potsherd is one of the archaeologist's best informants. Both the types of pottery and the figures that appear on them are non-Maya. At first, these foreign types blend into the Classic Maya style, but toward the end of the ninth century the change becomes more abrupt, which may indicate conquest by a non-Maya people. At nearby Seibal many of the stelae show a strong Mexican influence, including gods and motifs—such as the serpent and the speech-scroll—that are identified with central Mexico. These monuments are dated between A.D. 751 and 869.

Altar de Sacrificios seems to have flourished throughout the Classic period, until about 771, when it began to decline as a center and Mexican influence became more pronounced. Seibal existed as a site during the Middle Pre-Classic period but does not seem to have been important in the Classic period until after 751; thus it would seem that Seibal rose in importance as Altar de Sacrificios declined. Seibal is located on several steep hills, and one cannot help thinking that perhaps one of the chief reasons for Seibal's late flourishing was that it was located in what was thought to be a defensible position. Despite its hilltop location, it may have been taken over by the invaders, although the art of this late period is not entirely Mexican, but a blend of Mexican and Maya styles.

The reasons for the decline of the Maya civilization must relate to the entire Central area over a period of a century, because a local explanation for one site or another at a single moment in time is not satisfactory. The collapse of the Central area culture is all of a piece, and yet the last dated stelae appear over a hundred-year period; like lights going out one oy one, these centers died within this time span. It is tempting to search for a single romantic mystery, but to do so does not seem realistic. The factors causing the rise of the Classic Maya civilization in the Lowlands were complex and mysterious, and this must be equally true of the decline.

One may imagine a network of causes. The earlier decline of Teotihuacán and Monte Albán weakened the total fiber of Mesoamerica, but the Maya area took longer to die. Surely one of the factors was the rising of restless, aggressive people in central Mexico who came into the Southern and Northern areas and probably disrupted trade and the complex structure of Central Maya society. This Mexican influence may also have affected the Maya religion, as is suggested by the Mexican motifs in the art of the religious centers. At this time the Maya population was large and dependent for its support on trade and a well-organized social structure, and when its peripheral areas were affected by outside peoples and events the Central area probably collapsed slowly, like a besieged fortress, its gods no longer effective, its economy destroyed. It has also been suggested that trade routes were changed, cutting off the Central areas, and possibly disease or crop disaster or some other ecological problems worsened the situation. Disasters rarely come singly.

But we still do not know why the area was deserted. Why was it unable to continue under different circumstances as the northern Yucatán peninsula and the Guatemala highlands did? The Mexicans did not take over the Central area and run it as conquerors, as they did in Yucatán and the Highlands, and in fact there is very little sign of their being in the Central area at all; it was simply abandoned, without any evidence of serious struggle or catastrophe. Apparently some of its inhabitants made their way to Yucatán. In most areas there was still a small farming population that continued to come into a center on occasion, although the center was no longer a going concern, but on the whole the cities were strangely still and inactive on all levels. The great period was over.

Although the Central area was abandoned, Maya life, drastically changed, went on in the Northern and Southern areas. In Yucatán there was a new flourishing of culture in the century following the end of the Classic period when a large invasion of alien people and ideas came into the area.

Chichén Itzá, a city in the center of the northern Yucatán peninsula, dates to the Classic period; many of the buildings one sees there today are in pure Classic Maya (Puuc) style. It has long been assumed that, in the tenth century, invading Mexicans arrived there, bringing with them the culture of Tula, the Toltec capital. According to legend, they were led to

RECONSTRUCTION DRAWING BY TATIANA PROSKOURIAKOFF;
COURTESY OF THE PEABODY MUSEUM, HARVARD UNIVERSITY

Chichén Itzá, prominent city of Yucatán.

Chichén Itzá by the Mexican culture hero, Quetzalcóatl, the "Feathered Serpent," who was called Kukulkán in the Maya area and is supposed to have conquered Chichén Itzá for the Toltec. Whether this means that someone by that name conquered it—for there are persons in history by this name—or whether it was conquered in the name of, and with the aid of, the Mexican god, is not known. Quetzalcóatl was the ruler of Tula and was deified as the god of the planet Venus and as a god of vegetation. The god was represented at Teotihuacán, and some centuries later appeared as a beneficent god in the Aztec pantheon. Legend has it that he was driven out of Tula by a rival deity and made his way to the Gulf of Mexico, where he set out to sea and disappeared. Eight days later he appeared as the rising planet Venus. Just how he came to Yucatán, or in what form, is not clear.

The art of the Toltec period at Chichén Itzá strongly resembles that of the Toltec capital at Tula. At Chichén Itzá, galleries of colonnades were built, with pillars in the form of feathered serpents, and there are numerous representations of Mexican deities. Atlantean figures supported altars; the standard-bearer figure was common, as was the Chac Mool, an ambiguous creature who probably represented a rain god; intertwined serpents on stairway balustrades, representations of eagles eating hearts, columns with low-relief carvings of warriors, a platform with a pattern of skulls: these are all motifs associated with central Mexico.

It has long been thought—in part because of the Quetzalcóatl myth —that all of the Central Mexican traits at Chichén Itzá were brought from Tula. However, sculpture found in recent excavations at Bilbao, on the Pacific slopes of Guatemala, resembles styles at Chichén Itzá and Teotihuacán, and has been dated to the late Middle Classic period. There is also recent archaeological evidence that some of the so-called Toltec buildings at Chichén Itzá are actually underneath Maya buildings. A new dating scheme for Chichén Itzá proposes that the first Central Mexican influence there comes from Teotihuacán and dates to the seventh century; this phase was followed by the Puuc architecture of the Late Classic Maya in the eighth to tenth centuries, and the Toltec phase in the eleventh to thirteenth centuries. If all this is true, it requires considerable readjustment of well-established ideas. The history of archaeology is essentially a series of such adjustments.

The Castillo—the great pyramid at Chichén Itzá—is not as steep as the Classic Maya pyramids. Unlike the earlier pyramids, it has stairways on four sides, and the temple on top is different—it is squarer and squatter and has no roof comb. Bishop Landa, writing in the sixteenth century,

Façade of Temple of the Warriors at Chichén Itzá, showing the rain-god decoration in the background and a serpent column. Prototypes of the Chac Mool figure in the foreground have been found at Tula.

described the Castillo as a temple dedicated to Kukulkán. The construction of the Castillo, however, also seems to relate to the ancient Maya obsession with the calendar, for each stairway has 91 steps, making a total of 364 steps in the four staircases, which, counting the platform at the top of the pyramid, equals the total number of days in the solar year. Each side of the pyramid has nine stepped terraces divided by a stairway, for a total of eighteen sections on each side, the number of months in the Maya calendar. The nine terraces have fifty-two panels, the number of years in the Calendar Round, which was used by the Maya and probably also by the Toltec. This pyramid, like many others in the Maya area, was built over an earlier one, and it is possible to enter a tunnel dug by archaeologists and climb the lower steps into the heart of the later pyramid.

The period of Toltec domination, with its merging of Maya and Toltec cultures, was the heyday of Chichén Itzá. It was the time of the greatest amount of building there and of the production of much sculpture and painting. It is impressive as a new phase in the history of a

The Castillo at Chichén Itzá.

PHOTOGRAPH COURTESY OF THE PEABODY MUSEUM, HARVARD UNIVERSITY

Maya site, and yet the activity was not up to the standards of the great cities in the Classic period. There are virtually no hieroglyphic texts. The ornate elegance of Classic Maya art had vanished, and the art is plainer, harsher, more barbaric. Since the Toltec were not the architects the Maya were, many of the later buildings at Chichén Itzá had structural faults that caused them to collapse. Toltec architects continued to use the corbel vault, but instead of building the heavy interior walls of Maya buildings, they constructed lines of columns on which wooden beams were placed to hold the vaults; most of the beams eventually rotted and the roofs collapsed.

The Toltec domination of Chichén Itzá lasted for over two hundred years, and during this time it was the most important city on the Yucatán

Pyramid at Tula, the Toltec capital in central Mexico.

PHOTOGRAPH COURTESY OF MICHAEL D. COE

peninsula. Afterward it ceased to be an important center, but it was still a place of pilgrimage. At the site there are two important cenotes, the large natural reservoirs that dot the Yucatán peninsula. One was used as a water supply by the city; the other, the Sacred Cenote, was reserved for sacrifices to propitiate the rain god and to make divinations about the coming year's crops. Both people and objects were offered to the cenote for this purpose, and ever since the time of the Conquest there have been stories of beautiful young virgins who were thrown into the cenote. However, this seems to be more romance than fact, because, of the forty-two identifiable skeletal remains recovered from the cenote in the early part of this century, only eight were of women.

It is not known exactly when the practice of pilgrimages to the cenote began, but they continued even after the Spanish Conquest. Some of the carved jades found there were of Classic workmanship and it is possible that they were thrown in during the Classic period, but it is more likely that they were valuable heirlooms offered to the god at a later time. Most of the finds there date from a very late period—the thirteenth to the sixteenth centuries—and so it would seem that the practice of making offerings started late. The earliest pottery remains from the

PHOTOGRAPH COURTESY OF THE PEABODY MUSEUM, HARVARD UNIVERSITY

The Temple of the Warriors at Chichén Itzá.

cenote tend to be of utilitarian types, suggesting that it was used as a water source in early post-Classic times, but the later pottery tends to be ceremonial, indicating that offerings began late. The items found, in addition to jade objects, were worked bone and shell, fragments of cotton cloth and basketry, pottery, wooden spear throwers, figures and ornaments of wood, figures of copal and rubber, and hundreds of pieces of copper and gold, including plaques, masks, necklaces, rings, ear plugs, lip plugs, pendants, buttons, axes, arrow points, cups, bells, and copper soles for sandals.

Metalworking did not appear in Mesoamerica until the middle of the tenth century. Although metal had been worked in the central Andes for a thousand years before Christ, it took millennia to diffuse the techniques northward. According to native legend in Yucatán, metalworking was introduced into Mexico by the Toltec, but no metal objects have been recorded in Tula, the Toltec capital. Metal objects found in the Maya

The Sacred Cenote at Chichén Itzá.

area were hammered or cast, and sometimes welded. The method of casting was the "lost-wax" process, the same method that was used in the Old World, in which a wax version of the object is encased in a mold with holes at the top and bottom so that when the molten gold is poured in it replaces the wax. Hammering was often done over a mold.

Yucatán itself has no metal ores. Although some of the objects from the cenote are of Maya-Toltec style, the metal came from elsewhere. Aztec tribute lists tell that gold payments came from Oaxaca and Guerrero, and these were quite possibly the sources of the metal from which some of the objects found in the cenote were made. Other objects were clearly made in quite remote places. For example, one pendant came from Colombia in South America, and a number of other objects—figure pendants, bells, frogs, monkeys, jaguar heads, and other effigy pieces—came from Panama, while still others came from Costa Rica. The largest group of objects from the cenote are made of various kinds of copper and copper alloys. Gold objects were "killed" before they were thrown in—that is, they were beaten out of shape or crumpled—but the cast copper objects were offered intact. Many of the copper objects were bells, which probably came from central Mexico, and certainly the copper itself came from central Mexico.

Worked turquoise, which was considered almost as valuable as jade, also appeared for the first time in the area at this period. Fragments of turquoise mosaic have been found in the cenote, and other mosaic pieces have turned up in caches. Rock crystal beads also were introduced during this period at Chichén Itzá. Neither of these materials is indigenous to the area.

The objects dredged from the Sacred Cenote are clear evidence of the extensiveness of pre-Hispanic Mesoamerican trade and travel as well as of the far-reaching fame of the cenote cult. Bishop Landa writes that the Indians held the well of Chichén Itzá "in the same veneration as we have for pilgrimages to Jerusalem and Rome."

During the period that the Toltec were settled at Chichén Itzá, a people called the Itzá came to the Yucatán peninsula and settled at a place that was probably Champotón, on the west coast of the peninsula. The Itzá are mysterious people; possibly they were Maya from the Gulf Coast, although they were referred to as foreigners and some of their gods had Mexican names. In any case, they seem to have been influenced by a Mexican highland culture, although they were less civilized than the Toltec people. Around A.D. 1200 they were driven out of Champotón and came up the peninsula, and in the early thirteenth century they captured

Hammered gold disc from the Sacred Cenote at Chichén Itzá, showing a Toltec chief (on the right) pointing a spear at a Maya warrior.

Chichén Itzá. The city had previously been called by a name that is not now known. From the early thirteenth century on it has been known as Chichén Itzá, "the mouth of the well of the Itzá," referring, of course, to the Sacred Cenote.

At this time Chichén Itzá was the most prominent city in Yucatán, but, with the coming of the Itzá, monumental building there ceased. For a time the Itzá apparently lived peacefully with their neighbors. However, in due course the city of Mayapán became the dominant city on the peninsula.

Mayapán, on the western side of the peninsula, not far from the modern city of Mérida, had had a previous existence, but not an important one; there are no Classic Maya or Toltec-Maya buildings remaining there. From the thirteenth century until the middle of the fifteenth century, however, Mayapán dominated northern Yucatán. It was the seat of a centralized government exercising control over much of northern Yucatán—apparently not completely peacefully, however. The political state of the period is reflected in the fact that Mayapán was a walled city, whereas Chichén Itzá was not. There are also other walled cities dating from this period on the Yucatán peninsula.

The decline in the arts at Mayapán was even greater than at Chichén Itzá. The main pyramid temple, which was dedicated to Kukulkán, was a small-scale copy of the Castillo at Chichén Itzá. The ceremonial buildings were generally smaller and less impressive in design and were inferior in terms of both beauty and structure. The vaulted roof was apparently all but forgotten and was replaced by flat-ceilinged, beam-and-mortar roofs; stone was carelessly selected and crudely shaped and finished; rough blocks of masonry were covered by heavy overlays of stucco; and there was an increased proportion of thatched roofs on public buildings. Although the name Mayapán means "banner of the Maya," the art of the buildings reflects strong Mexican influences. Mayapán grew to be a city of eleven thousand or twelve thousand inhabitants living within an area of more than a square mile. The oldest part is the ceremonial center; the residential area grew up around it. Mayapán was the first city in the area that was clearly a residential city, not merely a ceremonial center.

It was at Mayapán that the bow and arrow first appeared in Yucatán, replacing the spear thrower, which had been the common weapon until that time. They are regarded as typically Indian, but were not introduced into Mexico until quite late, probably having been slowly diffused down through North America from Asia. The bow and arrow are said to have been introduced into Mayapán by Mexican mercenary soldiers. The Mayapán bow was made of hard wood and strung with a henequen cord and the arrows were made of reeds and tipped with flint points.

Mayapán had been under the rule of the Cocom family, but the city was overthrown in the middle of the fifteenth century by the Xiu, a group of people who had come late to the area and had been living in the ruins of Uxmal. After this time it ceased to exist as a peaceful center. There is archaeological evidence that Mayapán was sacked: charred beams and smashed incense burners have been found there, as well as skeletons with flint blades in them. When the Mayapán government was disrupted and the city destroyed, a number of small city-states were founded, which seem to have existed in a constant state of warfare.

The east coast of the Yucatán peninsula, however, although it has at least one walled city and evidence of war and incursions, seems to have been a thriving trading area during this late period, with boats that probably came around from the state of Tabasco, on the far side of the peninsula. The island of Cozumel, just offshore, was an important port of trade during the late period. The city of Tulum, on the east coast, still has a number of paintings on the walls of its buildings which reflect influences from Central Mexico, along with many Maya concepts. This area became much more important than it had been during the Classic period. When the Central area had collapsed, the peripheral regions gained in activity and importance.

After the fall of Mayapán there was never again a great Maya center. People sometimes lived in the old cities, but they did not build impressive new ones. Probably most of the buildings they constructed were of wattle and daub with thatched roofs. The most important of the late-period families were the Cocom, who had ruled at Mayapán, and the Xiu, and they were still prominent at the time of the Conquest and even into the sixteenth century, although never again did they have the power they had had in the past.

Archaeologists are constantly having to change or reshape their theories. For many years there was a belief that the Maya of the Central area moved to Yucatán at the end of the Classic period when they abandoned their cities, and thus the terms Old and New Empire came into being. Now it is known that Yucatán has a very long history of habitation and that it was inhabited in Classic and even Pre-Classic times, although it reached its greatest prominence in the Post-Classic period. Probably some people did go from the Central area into Yucatán at the end of the Classic period, but there was also a later Post-Classic movement back into the Petén. Whether at the time of the fall of Chichén Itzá or at the time of the fall of Mayapán—presumably in the middle of the fifteenth century—a group of the Itzá fled from Chichén Itzá to the area around the Lake Petén Itzá in the heart of Classic Maya country, where their descendants are still living today. In early Spanish colonial times the language of the Petén differed only slightly from that of Yucatán, although it was quite different from other Maya languages farther south.

The pattern of Post-Classic history in the Guatemalan Highlands was somewhat similar to that of Yucatán. Toward the end of the Classic period many of the valley sites in the Highlands were abandoned. Some of these sites had been occupied for over two millennia, and yet they were deserted, never to be occupied again, when people moved from these open valley sites to hilltop sites that could be easily defended and which were sometimes surrounded by deep ravines or protected by military outposts. They lived in a new pattern of close, fortified settlements and tended to move further away from the old ceremonial centers, disrupting the economy of the centers and leaving them with fewer defensive resources. Old religious centers were abandoned, and the new

Chálchitan in the Guatemalan Highlands, showing buildings with thatched roofs and a ball court in the foreground.

RESTORATION DRAWING BY TATIANA PROSKOURIAKOFF; REPRODUCED BY PERMISSION OF THE CARNEGIE INSTITUTION OF WASHINGTON

centers were as important for civic and defensive purposes as they were for religious ones; life became much more secularized and military. The new upper class boasted of their Toltec ancestry, for here, too, the new arrivals came into the area from the north.

As in Yucatán, there were changes in architecture and art. There were square-based pyramids with temples that had columns to form doorways and roofs of thatch or beam-and-mortar construction, and round buildings and masonry colonnades were typical innovations. Sunken ball courts were sometimes built that were open-ended with high walls and stairways leading out at either end. The stone ball-game equipment used in the Classic period disappeared, as the Mexicans apparently brought new rules and techniques for the ball games. Monumental sculpture was crude and showed the influence of Mexican styles and techniques. The Mexicans introduced idols, as they did in Yucatán, but the Chac Mool figures, the serpent columns, and the representations of jaguars so typical of Chichén Itzá are not found in the Highlands. Metal objects also appeared in the Post-Classic period in the Highlands, as did turquoise.

Maya life was permanently disrupted and changed after A.D. 900. In the areas surrounding the Central area, there are still many people who speak Maya, who have Maya faces, who have traditions that probably go back a millennium. But the Central area has remained permanently abandoned, mysterious, and still inexplicably lonely. In the entire area, there is a contemporary population of only 1.5 persons per square mile, most of them still clustered around Lake Petén Itzá, where they came after the end of the great Maya period.

IX.
THE BRAVE
NEW WORLD

Columbus reached the coasts of Central and South America and the islands in the West Indies on his voyages to the New World. He found people who wore little or no clothing, who had no permanent architecture, and whose only virtue in Spanish eyes was the fact that they had gold. Columbus did not touch the Mesoamerican shore, but on his fourth voyage, in 1502, he encountered a large canoe off the coast of Honduras. It was eight feet wide and must have been trading along the coast to or from Yucatán. The crew and passengers—a number of merchants, their wives, and children—were better dressed than any other natives he had seen, and the cargo, arranged under a canopy of woven mats, included an impressive array of copper plates, hatchets, and bells, flint-edged wooden swords, cotton woven in many designs and colors, shirts and cloaks, a fermented drink made of maize, and the ubiquitous cacao. The two boats drew up alongside each other, the Indians were brought aboard Columbus' ship, and Columbus and the captain of the canoe attempted to communicate—probably very unsatisfactorily. One only wishes that the Indian captain's impression of the oddly dressed men in their strange ship could have been recorded.

This was the first Spanish contact with the Maya world, and all that Columbus ever saw of it, for this was his last voyage. He died shortly afterward, still thinking that he had reached the East Indies, not realizing that he had glimpsed a civilization entirely unknown to the European world.

In 1517 a hundred and ten Spaniards in three ships under the leadership of Francisco Fernández de Córdoba sighted land—the Yucatán peninsula, a place that had never before been reported. The particular place was the northeastern corner of the peninsula. Bernal Díaz del Castillo, who was in Córdoba's company, described the encounter:

> . . . we sighted land, at which we rejoiced greatly and gave thanks to God. This land had never been discovered before, and no report of it had reached us. From the ships we could see a large town standing back about two leagues from the coast, and as we had never seen such a large town in the Island of Cuba nor in Hispaniola [Santo Domingo], we named it the Great Cairo. . . . On the morning of the 4th March, we saw ten large canoes . . . full of Indians from the town, approaching us with oars and sails. The canoes were large ones made like hollow troughs cleaverly cut out from huge single logs, and many of them would hold forty Indians.

The Indians wore loincloths and sleeveless cotton shirts cut like jackets and they seemed friendly, but when the Spaniards disembarked and walked with the chieftain along the road toward the village, they were ambushed by men wearing armor made of twisted strips of cloth who fought with lances and shields, bows and arrows, and slings and stones. Why this ambush took place is not clear, for the people of this coastal town must have been used to the sight of strangers and had greeted the Spaniards in a friendly fashion. It is possible that the Spaniards inadvertently antagonized them, or perhaps the Indians wanted to take the strangers as captives for sacrifice. However, there is another possibility: it was not quite true that the Córdoba expedition was the first Spanish contact with Yucatán. There had been a Spanish shipwreck off the Yucatán coast in 1511. Five of the survivors had been sacrificed, but two had been spared and were now living among the Indian population. When Cortés later came to the same coast and found the men, one of them joined the Spanish expedition. The other, who had adopted native ways, married an Indian wife, and become an important man in he community, refused to join his fellow countrymen and, in the ensuing years, having committed himself completely to the Indians, made a great deal of trouble for the Spaniards in their efforts to subjugate Yucatán. It is possible that he was the instigator of the treacherous ambush.

The Spaniards put the Indians to flight and continued into the village. There they found a small plaza with three masonry houses containing pottery idols, some of which they took to represent demons, some of them women. There were small wooden chests in these buildings containing idols, discs of gold and copper, necklaces, diadems, and small objects in the shapes of fish and ducks, all made of inferior gold.

"When we had seen the gold and the houses of masonry, we felt well content at having discovered such a country," Bernal Díaz commented.

So the Spaniards first came in contact with the people of the Maya area. They boarded their ships again, having taken two prisoners in the skirmishes before the town. Both of these men were cross-eyed, a feature that was considered highly desirable and had been deliberately cultivated in ancient Maya society.

Córdoba sailed on around to Campeche on the west coast of the peninsula. The northern coast of Yucatán was difficult for Spanish ships to navigate, as there are few harbors and many shoals. Navigation was simpler for the shallow-draft canoes of the Indians, which could be beached easily in case of storm. Díaz wrote that at Campeche

> . . . there was a pool of good water, for as far as we had seen there were no rivers in this country. . . . When the casks were full, and we were ready to embark, a company of about fifty Indians, clad in good cotton mantles, came out in a peaceful manner from the town. . . . They led us to some large houses very well built of masonry, which were the Temples of their Idols, and on the walls were figured the bodies of many great serpents and other pictures of evil-looking Idols. These walls surrounded a sort of Altar covered with clotted blood. On the other side of the Idols were symbols like crosses, and all were coloured. At all this we stood wondering, as they were things never seen or heard of before.
>
> It seemed as though certain Indians had just offered sacrifices to their Idols so as to insure victory over us. However, many Indian women moved about us, laughing, and with every appearance of good will. . . . At that moment, there sallied from another house, which was an oratory of their Idols, ten Indians clad in long white cotton cloaks, reaching to their feet,

and with their long hair reeking with blood, and so matted together, that it could never be parted or even combed out again, unless it were cut. These were the priests of the Idols, and they brought us incense of a sort of resin which they called *copal*, and with pottery braziers full of live coals, they began to fumigate us, and by signs they made us understand that we should quit their land before the firewood which they had piled up should burn out. . . . Then the warriors who were drawn up in battle array began to whistle and sound their trumpets and drums.

The Spaniards went back to their boats and proceeded along the coast. "As we were sailing along on our course," wrote Díaz, "we came in sight of a town, and about a league on the near side of it, there was a bay which looked as if it had a river running into it; so we determined to anchor. . . . This landing place was about a league from the town, near some pools of water, and maize plantations, and a few small houses built of masonry. The town is called Champoton." Champotón was the town where, centuries earlier, the Itzá had lived on their way to Chichén Itzá. The sixteenth-century inhabitants were the Couohe, the most warlike of the Maya. In his journal, Díaz wrote:

As we were filling our casks with water there came along the coast towards us many squadrons of Indians clad in cotton armor reaching to the knees, and armed with bows and arrows, lances and shields, and swords like two handed broad swords, and slings and stones and carrying the feathered crests, which they are accustomed to wear. Their faces were painted black and white. . . .

As soon as it was daylight we could see, coming along the coast, many more Indian warriors with their banners raised. When their squadrons were formed they surrounded us on all sides and poured in such showers of arrows and darts, and stones thrown from their slings that over eighty of us were wounded, and they attacked us hand to hand, some with lances and the others shooting arrows, and others with two handed knife edged swords. . . .

Feeling that our strength was exhausted we determined with stout hearts to break through the battalions surrounding us and to seek shelter in the boats which awaited us near the shore; so we formed in close array and broke through the enemy.

Ah! to hear the yells, hisses, and cries, as the enemy showered arrows on us and hurled lances with all their might, wounding us sorely.

Córdoba, the leader of the expedition, was gravely wounded in this battle, and died shortly afterward.

The Spaniards, having suffered great losses, decided to return to Cuba, but the following year "the Governor of Cuba, hearing the good account of the land which we had discovered, which is called Yucatán, decided to send out another fleet." This expedition, under Juan de Grijalva, consisted of four ships and two hundred men, one of whom was again Bernal Díaz. They sailed first to the island of Cozumel, again at the northeastern tip of the peninsula. Here the Indians hid from the Spaniards and would not come out, and Grijalva took possession of the island for the Spanish crown. Sailing along the coast again, the Spaniards saw a walled city that from a distance seemed comparable to their city of Sevilla. They then sailed around to the vicinity of Campeche, where Córdoba had been the year before. Maya warriors gathered, sounding conchshell trumpets and beating drums, and again the Spaniards did battle with the Indians, who, said Díaz, "were now very proud and haughty, many of them had their faces painted black, and others red and white."

I remember that this fight took place in some fields where there were many locusts, and while we were fighting they jumped up and came flying in our faces, and as the Indian archers were pouring a hail storm of arrows on us we sometimes mistook the arrows for locusts and did not shield ourselves from them and so got wounded; at other times we thought that they were arrows coming toward us, when they were only flying locusts and it greatly hampered our fighting.

The Indians put up a good fight against the superior Spanish weapons. However, the Maya were defeated, and after several days the Spaniards left again and began to explore the bay of Campeche.

On shore we found some houses built of masonry, used as oratories of their Idols, but we found out that the place was altogether uninhabited, and that the oratories were merely those belonging to traders and hunters who put into the port when passing in their canoes and made sacrifices there.

Farther along the coast there was a friendly encounter when the Spaniards gave the Indians beads, which the Indians took to be jadeite, the most precious of all substances to them.

> The following day more than thirty Indians with their chief came to the promontory under the palm trees where we were camped and brought roasted fish and fowls, and zapote fruit and maize bread, and braziers with live coals, and incense, and they fumigated us all. Then they spread on the ground some mats . . . and over them a cloth, and they presented some golden jewels, some were diadems, and others were in the shape of ducks, like those in Castile, and other jewels like lizards and three necklaces of hollow beads, and other articles of gold but not of much value. . . . They also brought some cloaks and skirts, such as they wear, and said that we must accept these things in good part as they had no more gold to give us, but that further on, in the direction of the sunset, there was plenty of gold, and they said, "Colua, Colua, Méjico, Méjico. . . ."

And so the Spaniards first heard of the marvelous city of Tenochtitlán, the Aztec capital, the present-day Mexico City, whose richness was to astonish them much more than did that of the Maya area. They then went back along the coast, debarking only for water, and returned to Cuba.

Hernan Cortés was in charge of the third expedition, which included this time eleven ships, five hundred men, and horses. In 1519 the Spaniards touched again at Cozumel Island, proceeded along the coast to Veracruz, and then went inland to the Aztec capital. After conquering the Aztec in 1521, Cortés sent one of his fiercest captains, Pedro de Alvarado, southward. In 1523 Alvarado subdued the southern part of Guatemala, the Highland Maya area. The conquest of Mexico distracted attention from Yucatán, and for a while the peninsula—which at that time was thought to be a great island—was forgotten.

Meanwhile, in 1524 Cortés set out from Mexico City to march overland to Honduras. Bernal Díaz was in his company of 230 Spaniards and 3,000 Mexican Indians, including the Aztec emperor himself. The route

Messengers of the Aztec emperor Moctezuma presenting gifts to Cortés.

lay through the heart of the Maya country, and the company had a
difficult progress through the jungle in the rainy season, fighting mud and
dense vegetation and having to traverse swamps and rivers. They built
bridges, rafts, and, when they could get them, floats made with native
dugouts. Indians abandoned their villages when word came of the coming of Cortés and the Aztec, and the problem of acquiring food became
critical. At one point, Cortés, fearing treachery on the difficult journey,
had the Aztec emperor hanged from the branch of a tree.

One day scouts came back with word of a great lake and a city on an
island in its center. Its houses and chapels were whitewashed and could
be seen from far away. This was Lake Petén Itzá, where many of the Itzá
had fled in the late pre-Conquest period and where more Maya would
flee before the Conquest was over. In fact, this town, that is today called
Flores, and is the capital of the modern Department of the Petén, was

FROM *Historia de las Cosas de Nueva España,* BY BERNARDINO DE SAHAGUN

the last of the Maya area to be conquered by the Spaniards. It maintained its freedom until the end of the seventeenth century.

Cortés went across the lake to the town, where he was well received and given food and objects of inferior gold. When he departed he gave orders to leave his horse behind because it had injured its leg, and it was left in the care of the townspeople. The Maya not only had never seen a horse before, but they had no domesticated animals and had never encountered an animal as large as a horse. In the battles between the Spaniards and the Indians the horse must have been one of the most fearful spectacles and one of the most important strategic aids the Spaniards had, as awesome a weapon as their gunpowder. The Indians persisted in believing that the horse and its rider were one marvelous creature, even though they sometimes saw them separately.

The horse left behind by Cortés was taken immediately to one of the temples. The Indians believed this creature that had been left in their charge by the chief who with his guns could create thunder and lightning and death was the god of thunder, for they believed that the sounds of the Spanish muskets were actually the voices of horses. They brought the horse offerings of fruits and honey and flowers and meat and birds. Not surprisingly, the horse soon died. The citizens of the town had a stone-and-mortar image made of the horse, and the image became an object of veneration. A hundred years later two missionary fathers found the statue being worshiped as the principal deity of the town, and piously smashed it. It has been said that on a clear day the statue of the horse can be seen at the bottom of the lake, although in recent underwater archaeological investigations no trace of the horse has been found. Undoubtedly it lies in rocky fragments on the rocky lake bottom.

In 1526 Francisco de Montejo, who had been an important captain under Grijalva and Cortés, petitioned the Crown for the right to occupy Yucatán. Ambitious to be a conquistador in his own right, he was one of the few Spaniards to realize that Yucatán—which he still believed to be a large island—might offer riches comparable to those found in other parts of the New World. He was granted this authority, and since conquistadors had to finance and equip their own expeditions, Montejo, who had already made money in the New World (and had also married a rich widow in Spain), set about to do this. In June of 1527 he was ready.

In September he dropped anchor off Cozumel, where the natives, accustomed to the Spanish by now, were friendly. He then crossed to the mainland and took possession of the land for the King of Castile. He founded a town and built Mayalike houses, but food was inadequate and Montejo was forced to coerce the Indians into giving his men food. There was still not enough food, and the natives grew angry at Montejo's further demands. The Maya were by nature generous and hospitable people and food was always shared with the stranger or the visitor, no matter how little there was. But the demands of the large number of Spaniards must have greatly strained the resources of the neighborhood. The place was hot and swampy, but although the men gradually became used to the climate and the situation improved, that winter Montejo pressed on to find a better place.

Generally the advance was peaceful, but sometimes, according to the *Relación de Mérida*, the Indians "would surround the Spaniards on the roads close to their pueblos where the roads were most thickly hemmed in by bush and would construct palisades which they interwove and tied up with the trees of the bush itself. . . . Then, when the Spaniards had entered . . . the Indians shot arrows at them with their bows from all sides . . . and they would launch lances, darts, and stones and everything else they had that could cause injury."

The armor worn by the Indians was made of twisted strips of cotton cloth, rolled and wound around the body, and some of this armor was so effective that arrows could not penetrate it. The Spaniards also adopted this quilted cotton armor for themselves and their horses, finding it effective against the native weapons and more suitable for this kind of warfare than their own steel armor.

To show ferocity and to appear fiercer and more valiant, the natives painted their noses and their faces around their eyes, and all the rest of the face, body and arms and legs, black or red [the *Relacion* reports]. The ears were perforated and small tubes which had pendants made of metal like tin plate, the color of gold, were placed in them. They wore their hair long, like women, and when they fought some let their hair flow loosely, while others tied it up in different manners as each thought would make him seem more fierce.

The Spaniards made their way slowly along the north coast. They were often impressed by the masonry architecture and were often welcomed and given gifts, occasionally a gift of gold that made them feel that real treasure must be just ahead. Always the Spaniards were seeking gold, although they did not realize for a long time that there was no less likely place to look for it than Yucatán.

After considerable exploration and the claiming of fealty for the Spanish king, Montejo sailed again from the town he had originally set up and went around to Tabasco, which had been a trouble spot for the Spaniards. It seemed to Montejo that Tabasco was the best base for his excursions into Yucatán and, in the spring of 1529, he set about to subjugate it. Here he confronted warrior chiefs wearing helmets plated with gold leaf and carrying shields covered with colored feathers and a gold plaque in the center. Many of these warriors also wore jaguar, cougar, and deer skins. But despite their fierceness, within a year Montejo felt he had accomplished his task.

The Spaniards then settled a colony at Campeche, but since Montejo still wanted to conquer the east coast, he sent his lieutenant to try to subjugate the town that had the best harbor. Here the fighting was hard indeed. The Indians apparently were led, or advised, by that same Spaniard who had been shipwrecked and refused to rejoin his countrymen, and eventually the Spaniards were driven out. They left by sea and headed down toward Honduras, making forays inland when food ran short. Many times during this journey the Spaniards encountered large trading canoes like the ones Columbus had seen, plying the waters between Yucatán and Honduras.

The Indians in the north and west where the Spaniards had established their bases had been friendly at first, but they gradually grew hostile. The Spaniards held out, but they began to make other plans. Montejo's son led an expedition to Chichén Itzá. This seemed an ideal place for many reasons. It was strategically located and its great ruined structures—the Castillo, the Temple of the Jaguars, the ball court—could be turned into powerful defensive positions. The stones of its ruins could be used as the building stones for new buildings. Its two cenotes furnished a good water supply. Although the city was abandoned, there was a pueblo close by that was still a place of political and military importance. And the ruined city itself, once the greatest of all Yucatecan cities, was still hallowed ground and a place of pilgrimage, the center of worship of Kukulkán. There was, moreover, a prophecy that Kukulkán would one day return from the east, a prophecy which certainly affected the attitude of the Aztec emperor Moctezuma toward the Spaniards and which may have influenced Montejo in selecting Chichén Itzá.

Having established themselves there, the Spaniards, outnumbered and without supply lines, tried to win the Indians over by peaceful methods, but the people became increasingly resentful. Landa states that the Indians felt "it was unjust for them to serve strangers where they were lords." Eventually there was a revolt and the Indians denied the Spaniards supplies, making it necessary for the Spaniards to go out and gather food with weapons in their hands.

The Indians found that they could defend their pueblos against the raids of the Spaniards and could blockade the Spaniards within their city by threatening them with starvation. Their confidence grew until in 1533 the Indians turned to massive warfare. The Spaniards withstood the first assault, for the defenses of Chichén Itzá—at this time called Ciudad Real—were strong. Early in 1534 the desperate Spaniards attempted an attack, but were defeated and retreated back into the city. The only thing left was to try to slip through the Maya lines and retreat to their allies on the north coast, from there to rejoin Montejo at Campeche. They completed their arrangements for withdrawal, and when darkness fell—the Maya never fought at night—the Spaniards silently began to leave the city. There is a story that they devised a clever stratagem to deceive the Indians into thinking that they were still there. They tied a hungry dog to the clapper of a bell and put food just beyond the dog's reach. The ringing caused by the dog's attempts to get food were taken by the Indians either as the sound of an alert sentry or the sound of the bell summoning the Spaniards to prayer, for the Maya knew by now that the Spaniards always prayed to their god before going into battle. The Spaniards slipped silently through a gap in the Maya lines and by daybreak were well on their way to the coast. In the morning the Maya, realizing that they had been tricked, took different routes to search for the retreating Spaniards. The group that found them gave battle, but the Spaniards turned them back and continued safely to the coast.

Although a wide area of Yucatán was more or less under Spanish domination by the beginning of 1533, the fall of Chichén Itzá made Montejo realize that his colonization was much less firmly grounded than he had hoped. In the spring of 1534 another city was established as the proposed administrative capital of Yucatán—this time a city on the coast.

Montejo had many problems to face in his attempt to conquer Yucatán: unfriendly Indians, a difficult coastline, a difficult climate and terrain, and the disillusion of his soldiers with the poverty of Yucatán, for they were now hearing of Pizzaro's exploits in gold-rich Peru. Colonists and soldiers began to abandon Yucatán in the belief that they could do better elsewhere, and Montejo had to abandon the new Ciudad Real he had just established.

Montejo was discouraged and wished to give up completely and go somewhere else. "In these provinces," he wrote to the king, "there is not a single river, although there are lakes, and the hills are of live rock, dry and waterless. The entire land is covered by thick bush and is so stony that there is not a single square foot of soil. No gold has been discovered, nor is there anything from which advantage can be gained. The inhabitants are the most abandoned and treacherous in all the lands discovered to this time. . . ."

Montejo's men were primarily adventurers interested in quick acquisitions of gold and whatever other treasure they might find and had little interest in the agriculture that was all Yucatán had to offer. It seemed to them they were enduring hardships for nothing. There were other problems in the conquest of Yucatán. There was no centralized government as there was in Mexico and Peru, where once the central government fell the country fell. It was more difficult to cope with the resilient separate cities that made up Yucatán, many of which were war-like and independence-loving. The Maya, when unfriendly, had a powerful weapon in simply passively refusing to give the Spaniards food and service. Many Maya cities had military organizations superior to that of the Spaniards. The Spaniards were individuals banded together for the purpose of conquest, while the Maya military organization was built into Maya social structure. There was a war chief of each Maya city-state who held the position for three years, which was for him a period of abstinence, continence, and relative isolation from his fellow man. Under him was a group of selected warriors, whose ranks were added to when necessary. The Maya knew their own countryside and its defensive possibilities; they were skillful engineers; they adapted well to Spanish techniques of warfare; and they had the advantage of greatly outnumbering the Spaniards. The terrain also worked against the Spaniards, who found movement difficult in the rainy season and the sun cruel in the dry season.

Montejo disbanded his forces and went back to Mexico City. In 1535 Spanish settlements were firmly established in Tabasco, Chiapas, Guatemala, and Honduras, but there was not a single Spaniard in Yucatán.

However, in 1537 Montejo's son began again the conquest of Yucatán. First he set up a base at Champotón, but the Indians again refused him supplies so he moved on to Campeche and set up a base there. This move was the beginning of the real conquest of Yucatán.

The Spaniards had learned valuable lessons from the first attempt to conquer Yucatán, and they did not make the same mistakes again. This time Montejo brought men who wanted to settle and raise crops, not those who sought gold and adventure. They began by settling near the coast, did not cut themselves off from each other, and established each settlement firmly before they went farther. They also learned to cope with Maya military techniques and to work at the rule of divide and conquer. In this respect, they were benefited by an increased enmity between the Xiu and the Cocom that had grown up in their absence. As Bishop Landa tells it:

> There was a drought, and as the inhabitants had wasted their maize in the wars with the Spaniards, such a famine befell them that they were forced to eat the bark of trees, especially of one which they call kumche, the inside of which is soft and tender. And on account of this famine, the Xiu, who are the lords of Mani, resolved to offer solemn sacrifice to their idols, and brought slaves of both sexes to throw into the well of Chichén Itzá. And they were obliged to pass by the town of the Cocom lords, who were their declared enemies, and thinking that at such a time they would not renew their old quarrels, they sent to ask permission to go through their lands; and the Cocom deceived them by a kind answer, and giving them lodging all together in a large house, they set it on fire and killed those who escaped.

The bitterness aroused by this incident made the Xiu seek the Spaniards as allies against the Cocom.

By the middle of 1542 the present-day city of Mérida had been firmly established and the Spaniards controlled the northern and western coastal areas.

But this was not the end. The Spaniards gradually worked their way east and down into the interior. Fighting was bitter, but they gained ground, although they fell ill and some died of disease during the rainy season along the insect-infested coast. The Montejos had tried to win over the Indians as peacefully as possible, but the conquest of the eastern part of the peninsula fell into the hands of other Spaniards, two brothers named Pacheco, who finally conquered the area around Chetumal with such cruel and violent barbarism as to shock even the toughest Spaniard. The Indians were garroted or thrown into lakes with weights attached to them, savage dogs were let loose to tear defenseless Indians to bits, and the Pachecos also cut off the Indians' hands, ears, and noses. The province never regained its importance. The area conquered by these people was largely depopulated by the ruthless fighting, starvation, and the abandonment of the towns. Again, many of the people went into the interior, to the region around Lake Petén Itzá, with its fortress town of Tayasal where Cortés' horse was still idolized in the temple.

Although most of the peninsula had now been subjugated, the spirit of many of its people was still not crushed. They had driven the Spaniards from the peninsula once, and they thought that they could do it again. Independence-loving and militarily efficient, the people were spurred on by their priests, who realized that the imposition of the Spanish religion would deprive them forever of their power. The plan for revolt was worked out so quietly that the Spaniards were not aware of it. The time for the uprising was set for the appearance of the full moon on the night of November 8–9, 1546, a date in the Maya calendar that was 5 Cimi, 19 Xul, Death and the End.

The uprising was to be coordinated all over the fringe areas of Yucatán. The eastern provinces acted on schedule, and with overwhelming fury. They killed, tortured, and sacrificed both the Spaniards and the Indians who had been loyal to the Spaniards. They crucified Spaniards under the hot tropical sun, used them as targets for arrows, or roasted them to death. The rebels even killed all the livestock belonging to the Spaniards and extirpated the trees and plants the Spaniards had brought from Europe. They tried to remove every trace of Spanish life and occupation.

Many of the chiefs of the northern area, however, apparently waited to see how things were going before they joined in, and thus the revolt was not unanimous or synchronized, although the fighting was heavy and bitter. Nevertheless, by March 1547 most of the revolt had been subdued. The eastern and southern provinces were reduced to a state of chaos and again many people fled to the region of Lake Petén Itzá. The Maya had put everything they had into this revolt, and after this uprising their spirit was crushed; they rebelled no more. The heart of Classic Maya country, the now desolate Petén and adjacent Chiapas, was not conquered for another 150 years. It was not until 1697 that Tayasal, the island town in the heart of the ancient Central area, was finally conquered.

In one sense, however, the Maya won out. At first the Spanish were determined to destroy the civilization they found and replace it with their own and were determined to wipe out the pagan religion and replace it firmly with Catholicism. But this was not as easy as they had thought. Maya culture was ancient, conservative, and deeply rooted, and the Maya had already shown their talent for silent, passive refusal. The Spaniards soon realized that they could only make compromises.

There were curious similarities between the religions of the Maya and the Spanish Catholics: both utilized the cross as a prominent symbol; both had altars and incense; both had rituals for the baptism of children and the confession of sin; both believed in fasting, continence, and the ceremonial use of fermented liquor. These things gave the Catholic missionaries a basis for conversion, a means of translating one religious meaning into another.

The Indians went along with the Spanish conversion and helped to build churches of poles and palm-thatch roofs. Before the Spanish arrival, writing had been a privilege of the upper classes, the priests and the nobles. Now, however, the peasants were persuaded to send their children to the missionary school, where they learned the Spanish form of writing. But while the Indians went to the schools and churches of the Catholic priests, they continued to give secret offerings in their fields to their gods of rain and fertility, as they still do. For the most part, the Maya have to this day not been completely converted to pure Catholicism. Pagan remnants are still strong. In remote areas one can find the image of the Virgin standing on an altar surrounded by offerings of chocolate and tortillas. In villages in northern Quintana Roo there are four small altars at the four corners of the plaza, each with a cross dressed in a native shirt. The sacred ceiba, the tree of life, is still cut and brought into the village at fiesta time.

When the Spaniards arrived in Yucatán, they found a hereditary aristocracy of Mexican descent. The peninsula was divided into approximately eighteen independent states. The usual pattern was to have at the top the *halach uinic*, "the real man," who was the political head of a state. The position was hereditary. The halach uinic had military, administrative, and religious functions. Under him, the *batab* was the head of each town. The batab was appointed by the halach uinic, although this was also a hereditary position—that is, the batab could come only from a certain family. The batab was often related to the halach uinic. The batab's functions were administrative, judicial, and military, on the town level.

The halach uinic and the batab had income from the land worked by their own slaves, as well as various official gifts and tributes. They received gifts as court fees, for example, and tribute from the towns. The tribute is said to have been light, however, and this was one cause of rebellion against the Spaniards, whose demands on the Indian economy were much greater than those of the hereditary leaders.

The noble class of the Maya seemed to the Spaniards to be parallel to their own noble class, and they did not try to abolish the system. In the sixteenth and seventeenth centuries the Indian heads of the towns were called *caciqués*, and they still had the rights and privileges of the old nobles. At first they were generally the same people whom the Spaniards had found ruling over the towns and provinces when they arrived. This custom of hereditary chieftainships seems to have lasted until the seventeenth century, when it changed more because of natural circumstances than because of Spanish pressure.

Landa tells us that

> Before the Spaniards had conquered that country, the natives lived together in towns in a very civilized fashion. They kept the land well cleared and free from weeds, and planted very good trees. Their dwelling place was as follows: in the middle of the town were their temples with beautiful plazas, and all around the temples stood the houses of the lords and the priests, and then the most important people. Then came the houses that were richest and belonged to those who were held in the highest estimation nearest to these, and at the outskirts of the town were the houses of the lower class. And the wells, if there were but few of them, were near the houses of the lords; and they had their improved lands planted with trees for making wine and they sowed cotton, pepper, and maize, and they lived thus close together for fear of their enemies, who took them captive, and it was owing to the wars of the Spaniards that they scattered in the woods.

The Spaniards were much impressed with the grandeur of the ancient monuments, most of which had been abandoned by this time. There were many stone houses in the coastal towns and fewer in the inland

Tulum, a walled site with small buildings on the east coast of the Yucatán peninsula, probably the city that Grijalva compared to Sevilla when he saw it from the sea.

towns. The towns were not laid out with regular streets, but each had four ceremonial entrances at the cardinal points of the compass and each entrance was marked by a stone mound on either side. A road led from each of these entrances to the ceremonial center of the town. Many Maya cities were fortified with walls or palisades. We hear of one that was surrounded by a living wall of the maguey plant. Some, like Flores—probably the ancient Tayasal—were on islands.

The first houses the Spaniards built were like the Maya houses, but gradually they began to build churches and buildings in Spanish style. Yet today the houses one sees throughout the countryside seem almost identical with those constructed over a thousand years ago.

The culture of the Maya area is now a mixture. Only a few years after the conquest there was a mestizo population in Yucatán, and as the people merged so did their cultures. The Spaniards, for convenience, adopted some Maya customs, and the Maya were forced to adopt some Spanish traits. Wherever the Spaniards settled they rapidly developed haciendas, raising livestock, horses, cattle, hogs, sheep, and goats. They imported plants from Europe and brought others from the West Indies, and yet maize is still grown as it has been for thousands of years and is still the basic staple crop and most important food. Ancient prayers are still offered in its fields, rites are still performed before the mountains in the hills of Chiapas, and copal incense is still burned in temples in Yaxchilán. Maya and Spanish, ancient and modern, are all mingled, but the strong tradition of the Maya endures.

Today the visitor to Lake Petén Itzá, whose islands and shores hold half the population of the large and lonely Department of the Petén, will find that Flores, the last citadel of the Maya, is a pleasant town, prosperous from the wood and chicle and rubber it sends to the outside world. Along the side of the lake there is an airstrip, and yet there are no automobiles in Flores and only a few trucks on the surrounding mainland. Flores is islanded not only by the lake but also by the jungle with its infrequent and muddy roads. Although Flores thrives in the twentieth century, the vast jungle around it is haunted by the strange ghost cities of the great period of the Maya. The main plaza of Flores is still decorated with remnants of ancient Maya sculpture, and many of the houses still have thatched roofs. The boatman who carries the visitor to the island uses the same sort of ancient dugout canoe that was used for centuries before Cortés crossed to the island—although today the canoe has a shiny new outboard motor, and the boatman may be wearing an Italian gondolier's hat. And he may tell you that on a clear day you can still see the image of Cortés' horse at the bottom of the lake.

A BRIEF
BIBLIOGRAPHY

ANDREWS, GEORGE F. *Maya Cities: Placemaking and Urbanization.* Norman: University of Oklahoma Press, 1975.

The Art, Iconography and Dynastic History of Palenque, parts I–III, Proceedings of the Primera and Segunda Mesas Redondas de Palenque, 1973, 1974. Merle Greene Robertson, editor. Pebble Beach: Robert Louis Stevenson School, 1974, 1976.

CHAMBERLAIN, ROBERT S. "The Conquest and Colonization of Yucatan 1517–1550." (Carnegie Institution of Washington, Publication 582.) Washington: 1948.

The Classic Maya Collapse. Patrick Culbert, editor. Albuquerque: University of New Mexico Press, 1973.

COE, MICHAEL D. *The Maya.* New York: Frederick A. Praeger, 1966.

———. *The Maya Scribe and His World.* New York: The Grolier Club, 1973.

COE, WILLIAM R. *Tikal: A Handbook of the Ancient Maya Ruins.* Philadelphia: The University Museum, University of Pennsylvania, 1967.

DIAZ DEL CASTILLO, BERNAL. *The Discovery and Conquest of Mexico, 1517–1921.* Genaro García, editor; translated by A. P. Maudslay. New York: Farrar, Straus and Cudahy, 1956.

GREENE, MERLE, ROBERT L. RANDS, and JOHN A. GRAHAM. *Maya Sculpture from the Southern Lowlands, Highlands and Pacific Piedmont.* Berkeley: Lederer, Street & Zeus, 1972.

Handbook of Middle American Indians. Robert Wauchope, general editor. 16 vols. Austin: University of Texas Press, 1964–76.

KELLEY, DAVID HUMISTON. *Deciphering the Maya Script.* Austin and London: University of Texas Press, 1976.

KUBLER, GEORGE. "Studies in Classic Maya Iconography." (Memoirs of the Connecticut Academy of Arts and Sciences, Vol. XVIII.) New Haven, 1969.

LANDA, DIEGO DE. "Relación de las cosas de Yucatán." Translated by C. P. Bowditch. Edited with notes by Alfred M. Tozzer. (Papers of the Peabody Museum, Vol. XVIII.) Cambridge: Harvard University, 1941.

MALER, TEOBERT. "Explorations of the Upper Usumatsintla and Adjacent Regions." (Memoirs of the Peabody Museum, Vol. 4.) Cambridge: Harvard University, 1908.

———. "Researches in the Central Portion of the Usumatsintla Valley." (Memoirs of the Peabody Museum, Harvard University, Vol. 2.) Cambridge: Harvard University, 1901–03.

MARCUS, JOYCE. *Emblem and State in the Maya Lowlands: An Epigraphic Approach to Territorial Organization.* Washington: Dumbarton Oaks, 1976.

MAUDSLAY, A. P. *Biologia Centrali—Americana: Archaeology,* 1 vol. text, 4 vols. plates. London: R. H. Porter and Dulau & Co., 1889–1902. (Reprinted, New York: Milpatron Publishing Corp., 1974.)

MORLEY, SYLVANUS GRISWOLD. *The Ancient Maya.* 3rd ed. revised by G. W. Brainerd. Stanford, California: Stanford University Press, 1956.

PROSKOURIAKOFF, TATIANA. "An Album of Maya Architecture." (Carnegie Institution of Washington, Publication 558.) Washington: 1946. (Reprinted, Norman: University of Oklahoma Press, 1963.)

———. "The Lords of the Maya Realm." (Expedition: The Bulletin of the University Museum of the University of Pennsylvania, Vol. 4, No. 1, pp. 14–21.) Philadelphia: 1961.

———. "A Study of Classic Maya Sculpture." (Carnegie Institution of Washington, Publication 593.) Washington: 1950.

ROYS, RALPH L. "The Indian Background of Colonial Yucatan." (Carnegie Institution of Washington, Publication 548.) Washington: 1943.

SCHELLHAS, PAUL. "Representation of Deities of the Maya Manuscripts." (Papers of the Peabody Museum of American Archaeology and Ethnology, Harvard University, Vol. IV, No. 1.) Cambridge: 1904.

SPINDEN, HERBERT J. "A Study of Maya Art, Its Subject Matter and Historical Development." (Memoirs of the Peabody Museum of American Archaeology and Ethnology, Harvard University, Vol. VI.) Cambridge: 1913.

STEPHENS, JOHN L. *Incidents of Travel in Central America, Chiapas, and Yucatan.* 2 vols. New York, 1841. (Reprinted, New Brunswick: Rutgers University Press, 1949.)

THOMPSON, J. ERIC S. *Maya Archaeologist.* Norman: University of Oklahoma Press, 1963.

——. *Maya History and Religion.* Norman: University of Oklahoma Press, 1970.

——. *The Rise and Fall of the Maya Civilization.* 2nd edition enlarged. Norman: University of Oklahoma Press, 1966.

TRAVEL INFORMATION

The adjacent states of Yucatán and Quintana Roo, which form the northern Yucatán peninsula, are being developed for tourism. Many sites can be conveniently reached by tourist bus, public bus, or car from Mérida, the capital of Yucatán, and Mérida is accessible by air from both the United States and Mexico City. Uxmal and the nearby site of Kabah are quite close to Mérida on a main road. Dzibilchaltún is only a few miles out of Mérida, just off the main road to the coast. Labná and Sayil, although nearby, are more difficult to reach, and a guide is advised. Mayapán is also nearby but difficult to approach. Chichén Itzá can be visited in a day's trip from Mérida, or it can be approached from the other side of the peninsula, from the resorts of Cozumel or Cancún (these are islands, but Cancún is attached to the mainland, and there is a ferry that takes passengers from Cozumel to the mainland). There is now air service between Cancún and the United States. Tulum, on the east coast of Quintana Roo, is easy to reach from Cancún (by car) and Cozumel (by boat or by ferry and car), or it can be reached by car from Mérida. Cobá is not far from Tulum by road. There are numerous hotels in Mérida. There are also good hotels at Uxmal and Chichén Itzá, as well as on Cozumel and Cancún, and there are a few along the east coast.

Palenque is an easy drive from Villahermosa, the capital of Tabasco (which has air connections to Mexico City and Mérida), or the adventurous may go by train. Yaxchilán and Bonampak can be reached by chartered plane from Villahermosa, Palenque, or San Cristobal. There are no accommodations at Bonampak, and only primitive ones at Yaxchilán. Comalcalco is also fairly close to Villahermosa, and can be reached by road.

There is a museum at the site of Palenque, and there are also museums in Villahermosa, Mérida, Campeche, and Cozumel.

GUATEMALA

Planes fly into Tikal from Guatemala City, and there is an inn at the site; reservations should be made in advance. It is also possible to stay in Flores, or on Lake Petén Itzá. One may fly to Uaxactún, but it should be remembered that there is no place to stay, and air schedules are uncertain in the rain forest. Adventurous travelers can also fly to Sayaxche, where there is an inn, and go by river to Altar de Sacrificios or Seibal (which is also approachable by a primitive road). Quiriguá is on the Puerto Barrios-Guatemala City road (and railroad). Kaminaljuyú is on the outskirts of Guatemala City, and other Highland sites can be reached from Guatemala City.

HONDURAS

Copán is best reached by chartered plane from Tegucigalpa or San Pedro Sula; there is a road, but a long and not very good one. There are two hotels in Copán.

BELIZE

Altun Ha is about thirty miles, on a bad road, from Belize City.

INDEX